The current values in this book should be used only as a guide. They are not intended to set prices, which vary from one section of the country to another. Auction prices as well as dealer prices vary greatly and are affected by condition as well as demand. Neither the Author nor the Publisher assumes responsibility for any losses that might be incurred as a result of consulting this guide.

Searching For A Publisher?

We are always looking for knowledgeable people considered to be experts within their fields. If you feel that there is a real need for a book on your collectible subject and have a large comprehensive collection, contact us.

COLLECTOR BOOKS
P.O. Box 3009
Paducah, Kentucky 42002-3009

Book and cover designs by Karen Geary.

Modern Collect

Sixth Series

Patricia R. Smith

COLLECTOR BOOKS
A Division of Schroeder Publishing Co., Inc.

Modern Collector's Dolls

Sixth Series

Patricia R. Smith

COLLECTOR BOOKS
A Division of Schroeder Publishing Co., Inc.

The current values in this book should be used only as a guide. They are not intended to set prices, which vary from one section of the country to another. Auction prices as well as dealer prices vary greatly and are affected by condition as well as demand. Neither the Author nor the Publisher assumes responsibility for any losses that might be incurred as a result of consulting this guide.

Searching For A Publisher?

We are always looking for knowledgeable people considered to be experts within their fields. If you feel that there is a real need for a book on your collectible subject and have a large comprehensive collection, contact us.

COLLECTOR BOOKS
P.O. Box 3009
Paducah, Kentucky 42002-3009

Book and cover designs by Karen Geary.

Dedication

This book is dedicated to Kathy Tvrdik, who is not only a delightful, talented, and fun lady, but a *true* doll collector and lover of all dolls. We count Kathy among our true friends and as most people know, you can count *real friends* on one hand. Thanks, Kathy, for being there!

Credit

The majority of the dolls in this book belong to Kathy and Don Tvrdik.

Other credits belong to Hazel Adams, Gloria Anderson, Joan Amundsen, Sandy Johnson-Barts, Shirley Bertrand, Virgil Bertrand, Sally Bethscheider, Candy Branard, Kay Branski, Betty Chapman, Carla Cornell, Linda Crowsey, Lee Crane, Renie Culp, Sandra Cummins, Doll Cradle, Ellen Dodge, Shirley Dyer, Marie Ernst, Frances Faatz, Frasher Doll Auctions, Sally Freeman, Maureen Fukusima, Green Museum, Genie Jinright, Luetrell Hurd, Phylliss Houston-Kates, Jo Keelen, Ruth Lane, Kris Lundquist, Margaret Mandel, Patty Martin, Jeannie Mauldin, Marge Meisinger, Shirley Merril, Sharon McDowell, LaHunta McIntyre, Peggy Millhouse, Jay Minter, Dora Mitzel, Turn of Century Antiques, Lani Petite (photo by Leanna Daniels), Florence and Flip Phelps, Cindy Ruscito, June Schultz, Marion Schmuhl, Paul Spencer, David Spurgeo, Sheila Stephensen, Martha Sweeney, Pat Timmons, Patsy Underwood, Mike Way, Ann Wencel, Glorya Woods, and Mary Williams.

Foreword

The majority of collectors in the 1990s have been asking, "What should I collect?" The answer is always a question. "How do you want to collect … for profit or for fun?" We love it when the answer is for fun, because that is collecting at its best. The collecting field can be very interesting and without a doubt enjoyable. It is also true that most collectors do answer "I want an investment doll," which means they want to know what dolls to buy that will prove to make a profit in a year or two. In answer, one can only state the facts, and if an item is unpopular to the public, it will be collectible. That usually means the dolls that remain on the shelves all year and end up in outlet style stores. When dolls do not sell, their production is stopped at an early stage and a supply shortage occurs as time passes. Popular dolls that sell quickly and are restocked in stores are also being bought by collectors from retail sources at a discount price.

Any hobby is supposed to be fun. It is designed to relax yet excite you. To collect something means making friends in that field and sharing your finds with them. How many times have you laughed or nearly cried along with a fellow collector over some incident that happened? How many fun times can you remember sharing together? *That* is what it is all about!

There is nothing wrong with making a profit, or expecting to, but do not be disappointed if you do not. If you collect the older modern dolls and go for the perfect, mint, and original ones, then you know what amount must be paid on the secondary market and must come to terms that a particular doll may or may not have room for anymore increase in value. Many high dollar modern dolls have peaked and most likely will not increase in value. If you "love" the doll, you will not care. If you are in it for investment purposes, you would be better off playing around with the stock market, which wouldn't be as much fun, but maybe safer for your money.

There has not been many "exciting" new dolls in the market in the past few years, except for some artist dolls, but who knows what this year will bring? The main thing is collecting dolls as a hobby, and as the collection grows, a built-in investment factor will also grow.

Table of Contents

3" triplets made of plastic and vinyl with molded diapers and bibs. Comes with rocking horse chair and dresses. Made by A.B.C., 1989. Complete - $10.00.

19" "Baby Darling" made of vinyl and cloth. Sleep eyes and rooted hair. Marked "Alter Rubber 1961" on head. Clean - $30.00; soiled - $10.00.

Madame Alexander Doll Company

Dolls by the Madame Alexander Doll Company have always been collectible and always will be. They are one of the very few remaining American doll companies and retains extremely high quality dolls and clothes.

For an in-depth study of these dolls and the company, the reader may order *Madame Alexander Collector's Dolls, The World of Alexanderkins,* or *The Collector's Encylopedia of Madame Alexander Dolls* from Collector Books. These books may also be found at your local library as well as others on the same subject.

The photographs used in this book have not been published in any previous *Modern Collector Dolls* books but may have been used in the other books listed.

Collecting any dolls can be fun, but collecting Madame Alexander dolls is doubly so. The newer dolls are in a competitive price range to other makers, but the older dolls can cost a lot of money. No matter what is paid for a Madame Alexander doll, it is important to remember that the clothes should be original to that doll. Also, the face color of the doll should be very good and not faded from play, sun, or washing.

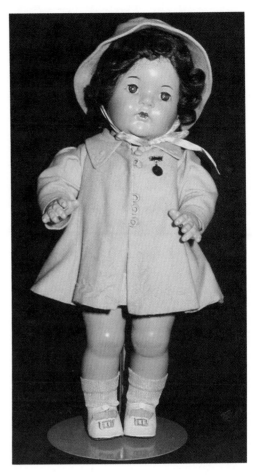

20" "Dionne Quint" is beautiful in tagged clothes and coat. The dress under the coat is sleeveless and came in various pastel colors. All original. $725.00 up.

7" "Dionne Quints" made of all composition and in original strollers. Pins are different; they have "Dionne" on each bar. Original. Each - $175.00; set - $1,200.00; in stroller - $1,400.00.

Another set of 7" "Dionne Quints" that are original and in original swing. They have the standard pins with the name of each girl on each pin. Each - $175.00; set - $1,200.00; in swing - $1,500.00.

7½–8" "Little Women" using the Tiny Betty doll. Made of composition. Has painted features, glued-on wig, and shoes and socks. All original. Ca. 1935. $275.00 up.

8" "Meg" and "Jo" from the Little Women set. All composition with painted features, shoes, and socks. Ca. 1935. Each - $275.00 up.

Left to right: 7–8" "Red Riding Hood," "Bridesmaid," "Scotch," and "Nurse" made of all composition. These original "Tiny Betty" dolls were used for Storybooks and Internationals during the 1930s. Each - $285.00 up.

7" "Tiny Betty Bride" made of all composition with painted features and mohair wig. All original except for missing veil. Complete - $275.00.

13" "Little Colonel" is all original except for shoes. All composition and uses the "Betty" doll. 1935–1936. $650.00 up.

13" "Little Colonel" using the "Betty" doll. All composition with closed mouth. 1937. $575.00 up.

21" "Scarlett" using the "Wendy Ann" doll. All composition with green sleep eyes. All original. 1937–1941. $1,400.00.

7½" set of "Dionne Quints" babies with bent legs. All composition with painted features and hair. Shown with book and two early teddy bears. Each - $175.00; set - $1,200.00.

14" "Sonja Henie" is made of all composition. Right arm bent at elbow. Body marked "Wendy Ann/MME. Alexander, N.Y." Tagged costume. $575.00 up.

18" "Dr. Defoe" is shown with "Dionne Quints" set. Dolls made of composition with painted features. Babies are all original. Dr. Defoe has added stethoscope. Quints - $175.00 each; Dr. Defoe - $1,800.00.

15" "Ballerina" made of all hard plastic and uses the "Margaret" doll. Outfit also came in blue, lavender, yellow, and rose red. Original. $550.00 up.

15" "Little Women" set made of hard plastic. Uses both the "Maggie" and "Margaret" dolls. Early 1950s. Each - $425.00 up.

15" "Story Princess" from NBC television show using the "Cissy" doll. Made in 1956 only in this rose gown. $675.00 up.

21" "Pink Bride" made of all hard plastic and uses the "Margaret" doll. All original with pale pink gown and veil. $700.00 up.

11

18" "Alice In Wonderland" with blue dress and eyelet trimmed pinafore. Wears hose and ribbon in hair. Uses all hard plastic "Maggie" doll from 1951. $600.00.

21" "Alice In Wonderland" is all hard plastic and original. Uses the "Maggie" doll and wears pink dress with organdy cap sleeved pinafore. 1949–1954. $750.00.

12" "Jo" using the all hard plastic "Lissy" doll. Blue floral with white bodice and sleeves and red apron. From 1965 set. $300.00.

12" "Lissy" in two outfits made between 1956 and 1958. Medium high heel feet, jointed elbows and knees. Both are original. Each - $375.00.

16½" "Elise Ballerina." Vinyl arms and jointed at elbows and knees. Also came in white and pink outfit. From 1957. $350.00 up.

12" "Brenda Starr" in original window box #975. All hard plastic with extra joints at elbows and knees. Sleep eyes. Set has extra hairpiece, curlers, and other items. 1964 only. Doll only - $200.00; in box - $285.00 only.

10" "Cissette" dressed in boxed outfit that could be purchased separately. Outfit also came in variations of color and in prints. Made in 1957. $200.00 up.

21" "Cissy Bride." Entire gown is overlaced. All hard plastic with vinyl oversleeved arms. Extra joints at the elbows and knees. Beautiful. Mint condition. $575.00 up.

13

10" "Cissette" in outfit #841–1958. This one is blue velvet, but the dress and jacket also came in satin. $200.00 up.

10" "Cissette" in outfit which could be purchased on the doll or purchased boxed by itself. From 1958. $200.00 up.

10" "Cissette" in extra boxed outfit. This one is dark pink but also came in yellow and blue. From 1961. $200.00 up.

Boxed coat and purse #0730–1963. This one is white with red lining and buttons. Also came in white with black trim/buttons and yellow with black or white buttons and trim. $200.00 up.

First "Wendy Ann/Alexander-kin." is a straight leg non-walker made of all heavy hard plastic. First side snap shoes had stitches around tops. $350.00 up.

8" "Alexander-kins." Both are all original bend knee walkers. Head turns as the legs move. From mid-1950s. Dress - $350.00; romper - $225.00.

8" "Bride," "Groom," "Bridesmaid." Bend knee walkers from 1956. "Bride" - $325.00; "Groom" - $450.00 up; "Bridesmaid" - $650.00.

15

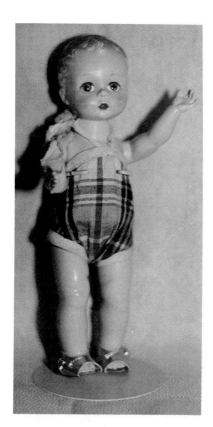

Left: 7½" "Quiz-kin" came with molded hair and wig over molded hair. Button on back moves head from side to side or up and down. From 1953–1954. $475.00. Right: Two 8" "Mary, Mary" dolls. Both have straight legs. Left doll is from 1976; right doll from 1979. Each - $60.00.

Left: "Amy" of 1987–1988. (There is a matching 12" in 1988.) $55.00. Right: "Amy" who is a bend knee walker of 1957. $200.00.

8" "Scotland" dolls. Both have straight legs. As shown, there can be a variation of plaid used within a year's span. From 1978. Each - $52.00.

Two of the many variations of " Mary, Mary." Both have straight legs and are non-walkers. Color of watering can can also vary. Left is 1982; right is 1975. Each - $55.00.

Left: "Scarlett" is straight leg, non-walker with pink rose print gown. From 1986 – 1987. $60.00. Right: "Scarlett" has bend knees and all green floral gown. From 1971. $425.00.

8" "France" is a straight leg non-walker. Was made in this outfit from 1985 to 1987. $52.00.

8" "Sulky Sue." Various prints used in outfit. Made from 1988 to 1990. $60.00 up.

"Little Women" set. Back row: "Amy," "Laurie," "Marme," and "Meg." Front row: "Jo" and "Beth." There can be variations of prints and trim. All are from 1987. Each - $55.00.

8" "Great Britain." There can be a variation of print used on scarf and width of black line on skirt. Made from 1977 to 1989. $55.00.

8" "Spain" made with this polka dot dress from 1986 to 1989. (Returned to all red gown in 1990.) $55.00.

8" "Panama" made from 1985 to 1987. $55.00.

8" "Tommy Snooks" Storybook doll made from 1988 to 1991. $55.00.

Left: 8" boy in blue stripe romper suit was a hostess gift made by Merilyn Moon for the Madame Alexander 1988 Convention. $100.00 up.

Right: 8" "Flapper" in red with white beads and gold purse was a hostess gift at the Madame Alexander 1988 Convention. (Maker unknown.) $125.00.

Left: "Flapper" with white outfit and maribou stole made as centerpiece and gift for the table hostess at 1988 convention. Outfits made by Joan Dixon. Three were auctioned at $150.00; fourth at $120.00. Right: This outfit was made by Judy Hernandez for the fiesta held the night before the 1988 convention began. Authorized convention souvenir with certificate signed by Madame Alexander Doll Club president, convention chairman, and two hostesses. $135.00.

Left: "Flapper" in pink with pink beads made for table hostess by Fran Clinkscale at 1988 convention. $125.00.

Right: "The Windy City" oufit made by "Bo-Peep" (Barbara Tipping DeMille) for the 1984 Madame Alexander Doll Convention. One-piece romper with deep mauve coat lined in same material and came with kite. Complete set - $275.00.

This doll has a yellow dress with blue trimmed Swiss lace overdress. Was second issue doll for members of Madame Alexander Doll Club only. 1990. $175.00.

Outfits in navy or red with white trim made for first meeting/symposium held away from Madame Alexander Doll Club Convention. Meeting in Atlanta, 1984. Outfits made/donated by Marsha Hunter and Pat Clark. Very limited. Complete - $200.00.

Left: 8" early Alexander-kin dressed in original Girl Scout uniform. (Socks not original.) Outfit tagged Jane Miller. $485.00 up.

Right: 24" "Kathleen Toddler" is made of all vinyl with flirty sleep eyes/lashes. Marketed in 1959 only. Marked "1958" in circle on back. $125.00 up.

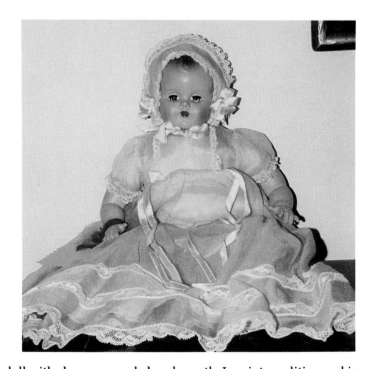

Left: 12" "Little Genius" is a cloth and composition doll with sleep eyes and closed mouth. In mint condition and in original box. Mint doll only - $225.00; mint in box - $300.00. Right: 15" "Baby Genius" is made of composition with cloth body and molded hair. All original and tagged. 1946–1947. $145.00 up.

25" "Pussy Cat," 16" "Pussy Cat," and 20" "Mommie's Pet." All have cloth bodies and vinyl head and limbs. 25" "Pussy Cat" - $65.00; 16" "Pussy Cat" - $40.00; 20" "Mommie's Pet" - $60.00.

15" "Patchity Pam and Pepper" are all cloth and original. Made in 1966 only. Each - $125.00.

18" "Funny." All cloth. Made from 1963 to 1977. $50.00.

Left: 14" very first "Muffin" with sapphire color eyes. All original doll with felt mouth. From 1963. $145.00. Right: 16" "Muffin" with yarn hair. Original. Made in 1965 – 1966. $175.00.

"Muffin" came with slant eyes from 1966 to 1970. Doll on right has eye change from 1970 to 1977. Both are original. Each - $110.00.

Left is "Muffin" after 1970. Doll on right is from 1966. This same doll was used as "Good Little Girl" in 16" size. Her companion doll, "Bad Little Girl," was same doll but eyes and mouth are turned down to look sad. Each - $110.00.

Left: 17" "Polly" in bright pink gown from 1965. $400.00.

Right: 17" "Leslie" with "Elise" face from 1970. Outfit also came in blue. $350.00.

Left: 17" "Elise" dolls. These outfits also came on the "Leslie" dolls. Both dolls are in mint in box. Doll in pink dress came with stole tied around head and has tan shoes. Doll in blue dress has stole around shoulders and has black shoes. From 1966. Each - $200.00. Right: 12" "Janie" toddler made of plastic and vinyl. All original. From 1964. $285.00.

14" "Mary Gray." Uses the "Mary Ann" doll that is plastic and vinyl. Made in 1988. $75.00.

14" "Pollyana." Uses the "Mary Ann" doll that is plastic and vinyl. First made in 1987. $75.00.

14" and 8" "Snow White" dolls using the "Crest Colors" from the movie and tagged "Snow White Walt Disney Productions 1975 by Madame Alexander. Exclusive Disneyland-World." 14" - $475.00; 8" - $475.00.

10" "Rosette Portrette" with a beautiful pink and black gown. Made from 1987 to 1989 only. $75.00.

10" "Flowergirl" Portrette wearing pink and dotted Swiss dress. Made from 1988 to 1990. $70.00.

10" "Anastasia" Portrette made from 1988 to 1989. $85.00.

21" "Melaine" of 1981. Will be marked "1965" on head. $300.00.

21" "Catherine de Medici" is made of porcelain. Limited edition of 2,500. 1990–1991. $525.00.

American Character Doll Company

The American Character Doll Company made some of the most desirable dolls ever. Everything they made was of excellent quality. The clothing, especially from the 1950s, was exceptional. The hard plastics dolls from the 1950s are highly sought, making them very collectible, because the supply cannot meet the demand.

Since the company began making dolls in 1918, they made many composition dolls. For general information, the composition "Patsy" type made by American Character is named "Sally." The early composition dolls will be marked "Petite." The later ones marked "American Character" and "American Doll & Toy Corp." are marked with the company name in a circle or straight line.

In 1968 American Character went out of business and all its molds were sold to other companies. Although the company no longer exists, collectors still have a fondness in their hearts and a prominent place in their collections for these lovely dolls.

24" "Sweet Sue" made of hard plastic with jointed knees and flat feet. Vinyl arms are jointed at elbows. Hair rooted into vinyl cap and placed in cut out of head. Sleep eyes and original gown. Gown also came in lavender, pink, yellow, and blue. 1950. Extra clean - $450.00; soiled - $225.00.

14" "Sweet Sue Walker" made of all hard plastic with jointed knees, flat feet, sleep eyes, and glued-on wig. Original gown with hair ribbon added. 1949–1952. Extra clean - $285.00 up; soiled - $135.00.

Left: 20" "Sweet Sue Sophisticate" is made of all vinyl with rooted hair, sleep eyes, and all original. Made in 1957. Extra clean - $385.00 up; soiled - $185.00. Right: 17" "Tiny Tears" is made of hard plastic head with sleep eyes and open mouth/nurser. Vinyl body and limbs. Romper possibly original. Marked "Am. Char." on head. $165.00 up.

Left: 17" "Toodles." Flirty sleep eyes with long lashes and open mouth. All vinyl baby body with bent legs. Original (missing shoes and socks). Marked "Am. Char." on head. $145.00.

Right: 10½" "Toni" wears gown called "Romance in Mink." All vinyl with sleep eyes and rooted hair. Made by American Character in 1958–1959. Extra clean - $165.00; soiled - $95.00.

19½" "Pittie Pat" using the "Butterball" doll of 1961. Rooted hair, smile mouth, and all vinyl. Key wound "heart beat." All original. Marketed in 1962–1963. Mint - $200.00.

29" "Miss Echo" is made of plastic and vinyl with sleep eyes. Plastic knob on front activates battery operated talker mechanism. Rooted hair, open/closed mouth with teeth. Uses the "Toodles" head. All original. Clean, original - $250.00; redressed - $100.00.

19" "Whimsie." Left to right: Unidentified doll, "Miss Take," "Blushing Bride," and "Lollipop." Dolls are made of all stuffed vinyl. All have original clothes. From 1960. $95.00 – 110.00.

"Herself the Elf" is marked "1982 American Greeting Corp./Hong Kong." Each - $12.00–18.00.

Annalee Mobilitee Dolls

Annalee Mobilitee Dolls are fun to own. They can add a look of laughter to any collector's home. Pose them on the kitchen window sill; have them peek from the doll case; even sit them daintily on the vanity in the bathroom!

The first tags were red woven lettering on white rayon tape. Around 1969 the tags changed to red printing on white satin tape. The tag became red printing on a gauze-type cloth about 1976.

From 1934 to 1963 the Annalee dolls had hair made from yarn. The hair was made from yellow or orange chicken feather from 1960–1963. Currently, hair is made from synthetic fur of various colors.

On older Annalee animals the tails were made from the same felt as the body. From the mid to late 1970s felt tails were replaced with tails made from cotton bias tape. Beginning in the 1980s tails were made from cotton flannel.

Right: 8½" monk with ski from 1970. 9" monk with ceramic jug from 1971. Both are felt with painted features and yarn belts. Each - $175.00.

Left: A cute Annalee snowman with top hat and pipe from the 1980s. $100.00. Right: 8" rabbit in Easter crate. Posable with wire running through body and limbs. Hand painted features. From 1978. $115.00.

Left: Large Annalee duck and basket from mid-1980s. $85.00 up. Right: 18" Ballerina Bunny. Only 2,315 were made. Tan flannel with blue polka dot tutu. From 1979. $250.00. 7" Ballerina Bunny. Only 4,700 made. Tan felt with blue polka dot tutu. From 1979. $150.00. 7" Ballerina Bunny. Only 6,013 made. Tan felt with pink net tutu. From 1980. $100.00.

Left: 10" clown with orange hair, pink/white outfit. Also came in lime green and orange (or pink). Only 6,383 were made. From 1984. $150.00.

Right: 10" aerobic girl with all felt body. Only 4,785 were made. Made in 1984. $150.00.

5" "Smurfette" made of all blue vinyl with painted features, yellow hair, removable shoes. Marked "Applause Div. of Wallace Berry Co. Inc. 1983. Made in Hong Kong." $6.00.

3" "Fred Flintstone" made of vinyl with cloth clothes and part plastic tie. Tag marked "Applause/Hanna Barbera." $13.00.

Left: 18" "Howdy Doody" with satin-type head and painted features. Cloth with vinyl glove-style hands and vinyl shoes. Tag marked "Three Cheers from Applause." From 1988. $85.00. Right: 13" Nintendo's "Super Mario." Cloth and vinyl with molded/painted features. Vinyl hands and feet. Made by Applause, 1989. $16.00.

Arranbee Dolls

Arranbee Dolls were some of the prettiest dolls made during the 1930s through the 1950s. They made the beautiful and delightful composition character child "Nancy" and a teen-style doll with a cloth body named "Debu-teen."

Their hard plastic dolls are a real treasure if found in an "unplayed with" condition. The basic name used by this company for hard plastic dolls was "Nanette," who came dressed in many outfits from street dresses to ballgowns.

The company was founded in 1922 and was purchased by Vogue Dolls in 1959. The use of the name "Arranbee" or the initials "R & B" was discontinued in 1960–1961. If you should find a hard plastic doll marked "Made In USA" on the back and "210" on the head, it will be an Arranbee doll.

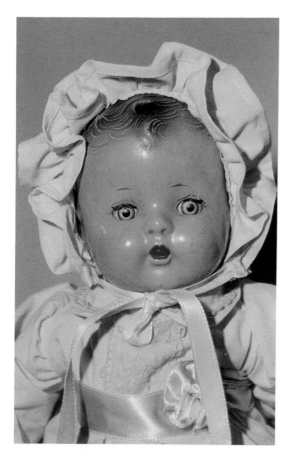

Left: 14" "Baby Kaye" has celluloid over tin sleep eyes, wide painted open/closed mouth. Composition head and limbs with cloth body. Molded painted hair. Marked "R & B" on head. Extra clean - $250.00.
Right: "Sunny Babe" is a large composition/cloth doll with smile mouth and sleep eyes. From 1936–1938. Extra clean - $300.00.

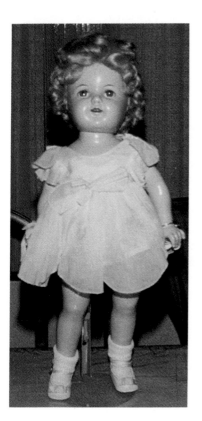

Left: 20" "Nancy" made of all composition with mohair wig, brown sleep eyes, smile mouth, and all original clothes. Marked "Nancy" on head. 1937. Extra clean - $450.00 up.

Right: 11" "Dream Baby" is made of all composition and is all original. Molded hair and sleep eyes. (Shown accidently as an American Character in Doll Values #5.) Marked "Dream Baby" on back. Clean and original - $175.00.

Facial close-up of 20" "Nancy Lee" doll in mint condition (never played with). Extra clean - $475.00.

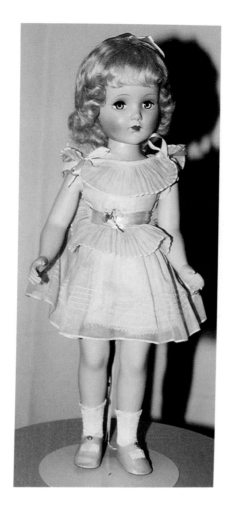

Left: 20" "Nancy Lee." Made of all hard plastic and in mint condition. Completely original. Marked "R & B" on head. Original box marked "Nancy Lee by Arranbee Doll Co." Extra clean - $475.00 up.

Right: 18" "Nanette." Made of all hard plastic with original clothes and skates. Walker, head turns from side to side. Made by Arranbee. Marked "R & B" on head. Original price tag marked $10.98. Extra clean - $325.00.

Left: 20" "Nanette" is made of all hard plastic and in unplayed with condition. All original and has matching umbrella. Floss-like hair in elaborate hairdo. Extra clean - $375.00.

Right: 17" "Nanette" is made of all hard plastic with floss-like wig, sleep eyes, and adorable three-piece outfit with wrap-around skirt, shorts, and shirt. Face color is faded. Doll is all original. From 1954. $225.00.

Above: "Kenzie Fashion Doll" made with jointed waist, closed mouth smile, and painted features. Original, came in box with two extra outfits. Made for Avon, Inc., 1990. $25.00.

Right: 11½" "Jenna Fashion Doll" with swivel waist. Came in box with two extra outfits. Marked "Created in China exclusive for Avon. 1990." Marked with only a "25" on head. $25.00.

20" "Mammy Yokum." Made of vinyl and cloth with molded hair and hat. Removable corn cob pipe. Made by Baby Berry. $265.00 up.

Left: 4" "Coke Kid" is made of plastic and vinyl. Has removable clothes with "Coke" on front. Marked "1986 The Coca Cola Co. Dist. by B.B.I. Toys. Made in China." $8.00. Right: 11½" "Coca Cola Girl" with painted features. Has jointed knees, ankles, and elbows and swivel waist. Head marked "1986 B.B." Made by B.B.I. Toys International. Made in China. $15.00.

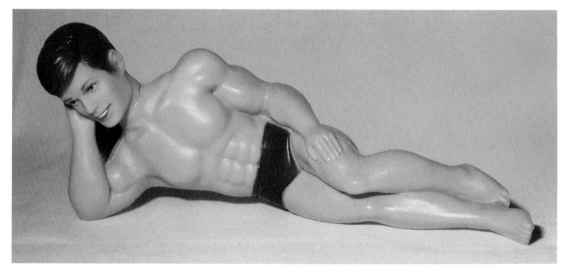

9" plastic and vinyl male figure. Molded in one piece with molded swimsuit. Side part hairdo. Open/closed mouth with two rows of teeth. Marked "Bakery Crafts. 1980. Made in Hong Kong." $42.00.

Yolanda Bello

There are 11 different "Picture Perfect Babies," all designed by Yolanda Bello and sold through The Aston-Drake Galleries, 9200 N. Maryland Ave., Niles, IL 60648-9853. The remaining editions of these babies have been closed in 1992. Retail is $63.00 to $90.00, but the older editions have gone as high as $160.00 as collectors try to fill in their sets.

16" "Michael" is made of cloth and porcelain and comes with baseball. One of the "Picture Perfect Children" designed and made by Yolanda Bello in 1984. Actually made by Knowles in China. Signed "Yolanda," with doll's name and number. $125.00.

14" "Jimmy" made of cloth and bisque with glass eyes. Comes with wooden train. Original. $125.00.

Betsy McCall Dolls

Betsy McCall was first introduced in *McCall Magazine* in May 1951. The cover of that magazine featured a little girl with her paper doll. On page 152 Betsy was shown as a typical little girl of the 1950s who lived in a white house with her mother, father, and dog, "Nosy." All the dresses in this first issue had the Cinderella label.

Many collectors are not aware that Betsy also had family and friends. Her father's name was James McCall. (No mention was made of her mother's name.) Her cousins were Barbara and Linda McCall, and her friend was Jimmy Weeks.

Betsy was shown with her own doll for the first time in the September 1952 issue. Clothes for the doll, which were from the McCall Pattern Company, were introduced in November 1952. Non-doll items for Betsy McCall were marketed within the next year. Dishes and silverware could be purchased at various retail stores in 1953. Macy's offered a Betsy McCall Halloween costume that same year. In November 1953 "Betsy, My Paper Doll" sung by Rosemary Clooney was released as 45 and 78 rpm records. In 1958 matching dresses for child and doll were designed by Helen Lee.

In 1959 Betsy's appearance was changed with another change soon to follow in 1960. In October 1961 the Betsy McCall doll took on an entire new look. By 1964 Betsy McCall patterns were no longer in the McCall pattern books and were replaced by Barbie doll patterns.

Doll Descriptions and Production Years

14", 1952: Vinyl head with rooted hair, hard plastic body. Made by Ideal. Marked "P-90." $300.00.

8", 1958: All hard plastic with jointed knees. Made by American Character Doll Co. Street dress - $175.00; ballgown - $225.00 up.

14", 1958: Vinyl with rooted hair, medium high heel feet, round sleep eyes. Made by American Character Dolls Co. Marked "McCall 1958." $285.00.

19–20", 1958: Vinyl head with rooted hair, slender limbs. Made by American Character Doll Co. $300.00 up.

29–30", 1959: All vinyl, rooted hair. Made by American Character Doll Co. $475.00 up.

36", 1959: Marked "McCall 1959." Made by Ideal Doll Co. $675.00 up.

36", 1959: Boy doll called "Sandy" but may be correct if called "James." Marked same as 36" girl. Made by Ideal Doll Co. $725.00 up.

22", 1961: Has extra joints at wrists, knees, ankles, and waist. Made by Ideal Doll Co. $325.00 up.

8" and 14" "Betsy McCall" made by American Character Doll Company. The small one is all hard plastic and the large one is all vinyl. Both have the same style dresses. They are all original and in played with condition. 14" - $185.00; 8" - $125.00.

29", 1961: Has extra joints at ankles, knees, waist, and wrists. Made by American Character Doll Co. $500.00 up.

29", 1971–1974: Plastic and vinyl. Open/closed mouth with painted teeth. Has long slender fingers. Marked "B.M.C. Horsman." $265.00.

13", 1975: Came in one-piece green/pink jumpsuit with "Betsy" on front. Made by Horsman, designed by Irene Szor. Head will be marked "Horsman Dolls, Inc. 1967." $65.00 up.

11½", late 1970s: Brown sleep eyes, reddish rooted hair. Made by Uneeda. $125.00.

BIKIN

Fairy Tale set of "Little Red Riding Hood." Includes 12" Grandmother and Wolf and 7" Little Red Riding Hood. Plastic and vinyl construction. Grandmother's face is wrinkled and has molded-on glasses. Comes with cassette audio tape of story. Made by Bikin Express Ltd., 1988. Complete set - $30.00.

Bikin Fairy Tale set of "Sleeping Beauty." Includes 12" Witch and 11½" Prince and Sleeping Beauty. Complete set with cassette audio tape of story - $30.00.

7" "Seven Dwarfs" made of plastic and vinyl. Made in China for Bikin, 1988. Complete set - $50.00.

11½" Bikin Fairy Tales dolls. "Snow White" and "Prince" with painted features. Marked "Made in China/Bikin/Disney." Each - $24.00.

13" "Buddy Lee." Made of plastic and vinyl with orange molded hair. Has original Lee overalls and shirt. Made in mid-1980s. $65.00.

43

Cabbage Patch Dolls

Original Xavier Roberts "Babyland General" or "Appalachian" dolls have birth certificates. Each doll "edition" has a different color/design on the border of the birth certificates.

Editions

Blue Edition: Name was "Helen" and less than 1,000 were made in 1978. $3,500.00.

"A" Blue Edition: Less than 1,000 made. Preemies referred to as "SP" Preemies. $1,300.00.

"B" Red Edition: These are first to have adoption papers. November 1978. $1,200.00.

"C" Burgandy Edition: January 1979. 5,000 issue. Registration number has prefix "C." $900.00.

"D" Purple Edition: 10,000 edition which was sold out by November 1979. $800.00.

"X" Christmas Edition: Edge of certificate has leaves and berries. Edition was 1,000. $1,200.00.

"E" Bronze Edition: This was last edition of 1979 and 15,000 edition. $600.00.

Signed Preemie Edition: April, 1980. 5,000 edition and hand signed. $600.00.

Celebrity Edition: 1980, 5,000 edition. All hand signed. $500.00.

Christmas Edition: 1980, 2,500 edition. Hand signed. $600.00.

Grand Edition: 1980, dressed in evening attire of tuxedo, diamonds. $750.00.

New Ears Edition: 1981, first babies with ears. Edition of 15,000. Signature is stamped. $175.00.

Cleveland Green Edition: Limited to 2,000. Sold out by February 1983. $400.00.

"KP" Darker Green Edition: 1983, 2,000 edition. $550.00.

"KPR" Red Edition: 1983, 2,000 edition. $550.00.

"KPB" Burgandy Edition: 1983, 10,000 edition. $200.00.

Oriental Edition: 1983, 1,000 edition. $850.00.

American Indian Edition: 1983, 1,000 edition. $850.00.

Hispanic Edition: 1983, 1,000 edition. $750.00.

"KPZ" Edition: 1983 or 1984. Bronze border, 30,000 edition. $175.00.

Champagne Edition: 1983–1984, 2,000 edition. $900.00.

"KPP" Purple Edition: 1984, 20,000 edition. $250.00.

"KPF" Turquoise Edition: 1984, 30,000 edition. $100.00.

"KPG" Coral Edition: 1984, 30,000 edition. $100.00.

"PH" Rose Edition: 1984, 40,000 edition. $100.00.

"KPI" Ivory Edition: 1985, 45,000 edition. $100.00.

"KPJ" Gold Edition: 1985, 50,000 edition. $100.00.

Emerald Edition: 1985, Edition size unknown. $100.00.

Coleco Cabbage Patch Dolls

1983: Dolls have powder scent. Includes bald babies, dolls with pacifiers and/or freckles, bald Black babies, Black boys, boys with fuzzy red hair, and white boys and girls. $75.00–150.00.

1984: Black and white boys and girls, preemies, dolls with pacifiers, and dolls with orange hair. $45.00–75.00.

1985: Twins, Black and white boys and girls, dolls with pacifiers, glasses, or one tooth. $50.00–95.00.

1986: Same as 1985.

Foreign Coleco: Germany, Canada, Spain, etc. Freckles, pacifiers, boys and girls. $40.00–60.00.

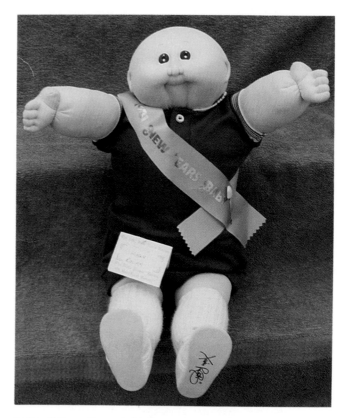

1981 "New Ears Edition" from Babyland General. $175.00.

Standing is 1983 Coleco #1 boy. Sitting is a 1984 #1 Black Preemie in rare knit outfit. Each - $50.00 – 150.00.

1983 Coleco #4 red and black shag haired boys. Each - $175.00 – 300.00.

Back row: Powder scent doll with red loopy curl. Made in Japan. 1983. Boy with black shag hair. Made in Mexico. Front row: Bald baby with freckles and pacifier. Made in South Africa. 1984. Boy with red shag hair and freckles. Made in Spain. 1983. Each - $125.00 – 200.00.

Coleco girl with double auburn popcorn hair. Made in 1986. Girl with "Cornsilk" hair. Made in 1988. Each - $30.00 – 45.00.

CABBAGE PATCH DOLLS

Cabbage Patch girls with dimples. One has single braid ponytail; the other has a ponytail to the side. 1985. Each - $35.00 – 60.00.

Left: Coleco baseball player. From 1986. Right: Black boy doll with glasses. From 1985. Each - $30.00 – 45.00.

Black doll with smile face and single ponytail. From 1987. Doll with champagne popcorn hair and lavender eyes. From 1986. Each - $30.00 – 45.00.

16" Coleco with grow hair from 1987. $35.00.

"Talking" Cabbage Patch by Coleco, 1987. $45.00.

10" "Babyland Kid" by Coleco, 1987. Also marked "A.A. Inc." $30.00.

Cameo Doll Company

Regular dolls made by Cameo are rare except for the "Kewpie," "Miss Peep," and "Scootles" dolls. During the 1920s and 1930s Cameo made some delightful characters such as "Joy," "Margie," "Champ," and many others.

In 1970 original Cameo Kewpie molds were sold to the Strombecker Corp. During the 1970s Joseph Kallus, founder of the company, retained some of the Cameo molds and issued them in limited edition under the name Cameo Exclusive Products. Kewpies marked with "S71" were made by Strombecker. Eventually, all Kewpie molds were sold to Jesko.

8½" "Pete The Pup." Composition head, segmented wooden body and limbs. Label on front. Made by Cameo. $275.00 up.

Left to right: "Little Annie Rooney" has tag with name and "Copyright 1925 by Jack Collins. Pat. Applied for." $700.00. "Giggles" with molded full bang hairdo, unmarked. $325.00. "Margie" has label on chest. Composition head and wooden segmented body. 1929. $265.00. "Joy" has molded loop in hair for ribbon and label on chest. Made of composition and wood. $350.00.

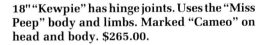

Left: 22" "Kewpie" is very rare celluloid with jointed shoulders only. Made in Japan. $500.00. 9" "Kewpie" made of hard plastic. Marked "Rose O'Neill." $185.00. 5" "Kewpie" made of celluloid. Marked in circle on back "Kewpie Rose O'Neill 1913." $90.00. 2½" "Kewpie" made of celluloid. Marked "10/0 Germany." Paper label on back marked "Rose O'Neill/1913/Kewpie Reg. U.S. Pat. Off./Des. Pat. 1114-1913/Germany." $45.00. Right: Shows the back view of the rare 22" "Kewpie" made of all celluloid.

18" "Kewpie" has hinge joints. Uses the "Miss Peep" body and limbs. Marked "Cameo" on head and body. $265.00.

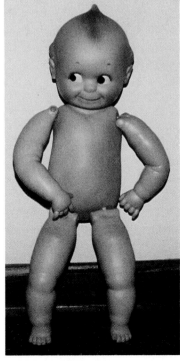

15" "Skootles" dolls. Both are all original and all composition. One has eyes painted to the front, and the other has eyes painted to the side. Brown-eyed doll has blue floral dress. Blue-eyed doll has red checkered romper. Each - $600.00 up.

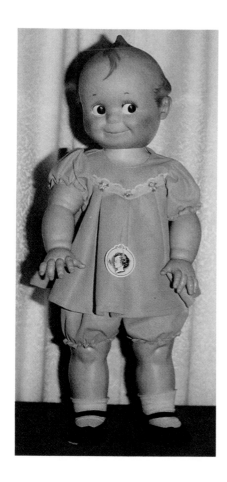

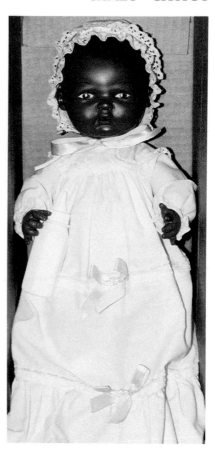

Left: 27" "Kewpie" made of all vinyl with jointed neck, shoulders, and hips. Modeled top knot and tuffs of hair. All original. $325.00.

Right: 18" black "Newborn Miss Peep" made of plastic and vinyl. Regular five-piece baby body rather than the hinged "Miss Peep" body. $60.00.

18" "Real Friend" is made of plastic and vinyl with sleep eyes, open/closed mouth, and rooted hair. Marked "Made in China/1986/Cititoy." $40.00.

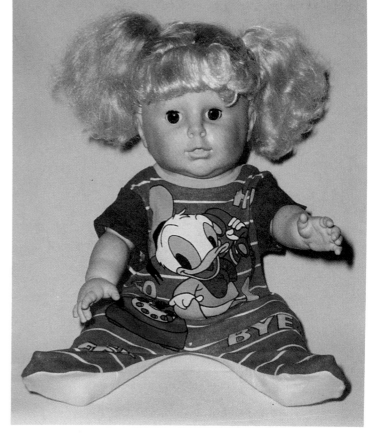

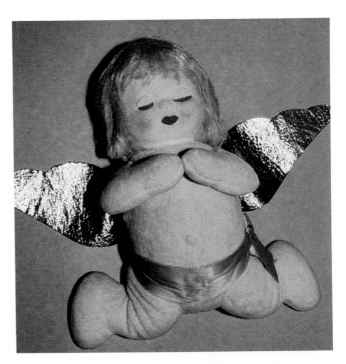

8" "Angel Baby Bottle Holder." Velvet with pressed felt face mask, mohair wig, and metallic wings. Music box in body. Tagged "Clare Creations Inc. N.Y." From late 1930s to mid-1940s. $25.00.

20" all cloth with yarn hair and embroidered features. Individual stitched fingers, painted features, and all original. Marked "Tes Ada Lum Shanchai. Made in China." Ca. 1930s. $50.00.

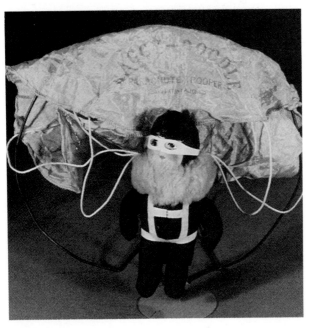

7" parachute jumper from World War II. Real fur around neck, oil cloth stitched head, helmet, and face mask. Separate goggles. Marked "Raggy-Doodle/U.S. Parachute Trooper/Design Patent Allowed." $60.00.

41" "Daniel Boone" with plastic face mask and freckles. Straps on hands and feet allow it to become "dancing partner" for child. All original, 1950s. $185.00.

14" cloth with mask type vinyl face with painted features and molded hair. Made in 1950s. $35.00.

11" "Mr. Flashmore, Jr." All cloth, sexed, yarn hair, felt eyes, and removable trench coat. Made in Korea by Wallace Berry & Co. in 1977. Tagged "The Flasher." $42.00.

Right: 12" "Bobby Snooks" made of all cloth with printed-on clothes and features. Has cloth storybook. 1980. Left: Reverse side of "Bobby Snooks" is pirate with bandaged nose. $15.00.

14" "Valerie," a Valentine cloth doll with yarn hair and painted features. Made by Kamar, Inc. $30.00.

14" "Sugar Plum" made of all cloth with painted features, yarn hair, and applied ears. Original. Tagged "Copyright 1988 Morgan Inc. by Amtoy." $27.00.

17" "Anne of Green Gables" all cloth doll. Embroidered face, large green painted eyes, yarn hair. Original, hand-made on Prince Edward Island, Canada and sold through The House of Green Gables Museum. Tagged "Anne Shirley/ Lovingly made by The Village Craft House." $85.00.

24" "Edith The Lonely Doll" made of all felt with painted features. Made exclusively for Rothchilds, a doll shop and dealer, 1987–1988. $100.00.

22" all cloth doll with yarn hair, printed features, and removable pinafore. Tagged "Calico Critter of N.J." $20.00.

17" "Taro Patch" has soft sculptured stockinette over cloth and painted features. Comes with passport that has glossy photo of doll in same dress. Original. Made in Hong Kong, 1985. $75.00.

12" "Prince Charles" with vinyl head and cloth body. Removable jacket only. Has suction cups on hands. Tagged "Made in Korea." $15.00.

17½" soft stuffed muslin doll with stitched joints and fingers. Tapestry cloth two-piece outfit and red corduroy removable slippers. Black yarn hair, embroidered features on nylon stretched over a plastic ball. Made by Taiwan cottage industry. $45.00.

"Gabby" is a cute all cloth doll with non-removable clothes. Made by Etone in the late 1980s. $20.00.

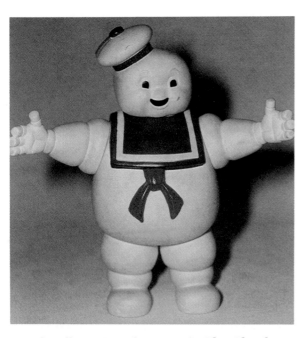

7" "Marshmallow Man" from movie *The Ghostbusters.* One-piece vinyl, unjointed. Molded-on hat marked "Stay Puft." Foot marked "1984 Columbia Productions." $18.00.

8" "Ginger" has bare feet and a round face. All original. Can be either a strung doll, a walker, or a vinyl head doll. Made by Cosmopolitan. $65.00 up.

8" "Ginger" in Trousseau Series #773. Gown may have come in several different colors. $85.00 up.

13½" plastic and vinyl doll with painted eyes. Marked "C.P.G. Products Corp. 1979." $22.00.

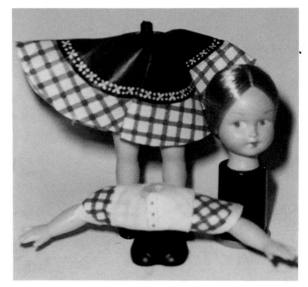

Left: 9" "Pop Apart" doll made of all plastic with painted features and rooted hair. Outfits come ready to cut and put on doll. Marked "Cragstan Industries, Inc." 1979. $20.00. Right: Doll shown as its different parts.

11½" "Flower Princess Ballerina" has snapping knees, arms molded in bent position and feet molded on toes. Painted features, rooted hair. Marked "1982 Creata" on head. $25.00.

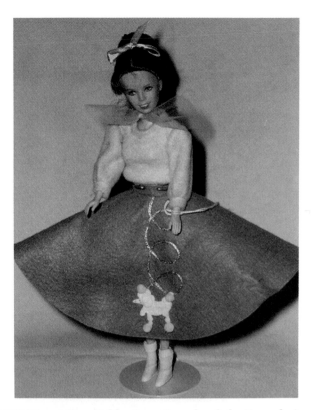

11½" "Peggy Sue, Bobby Soxer" made of plastic and vinyl with snapping knees. Marked "Creata 1986" on head. $38.00.

11½" "1952 Bobby Soxer" made of plastic and vinyl with snapping knees. Original. Marked "Creata 1986" on head. $30.00.

11½" "Teddy Girl" with bend knees. 1989. Dark hair dolls are named "Vanessa," blondes are "Heather," and redheads are "Tiffany." Marked "Creata 1986" on head. $30.00.

6" "Today's Girl" as one of the "Pony Gals." Lavender star painted eyes, rooted hair. All vinyl. Marked "1989 Creata." $16.00.

Left: 6" "Rose Petal" made of plastic and vinyl. Made by David Kirschner. Marked on head and body "DKP/1984." Other dolls in series are "Lilly Fair" in white short dress, "Daffodil" in yellow long gown, "Sunny Sunflower" in yellow short dress with scalloped hem, and "Orchid" (right) in purple/white dress. (Dress should be at her shoulders.) Each - $12.00.

8" "Basketball Dreamdoll" with molded hair, painted features, and attached basketball. Made by Dakin in 1970. $8.00.

Dolls are from the "Boys and Their Toys" series. Made of cloth and porcelain with glass eyes. All are original and designed by Elke Hutchens. Left: "David" with a wooden fire truck. Right: "Steve" with wooden tractor. Below: "Tommy" with wooden airplane. Made by Danbury Mint. Each - $95.00 up.

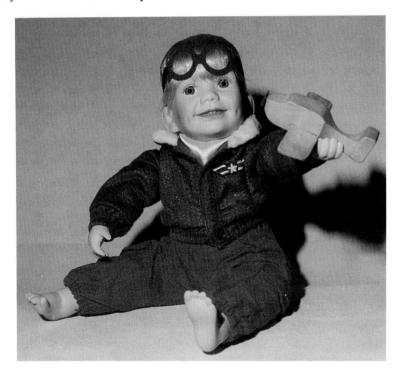

Deluxe Toys

Deluxe Toys was the parent company of Deluxe Reading, Deluxe Topper, Topper Corp., Deluxe Toy Creation, and Deluxe Premiums and was in business from the 1950s to the late 1970s. Most of the dolls from this company are battery-operated "action" toys. The most collectible dolls from Deluxe are "Dawn" and friends from 1970.

Right: One of the 6" "Combat Kid" figures from "The Tigers." Posable arms and legs. Made by Topper Toys. $30.00.

10" "Busy Baby Walker" made of plastic and vinyl. Battery operated. Uses the "Bikey" 1968 body and legs. Deluxe Toys, 1969. $16.00.

6½" "One Star General" with bendable legs. Hand holds gun. Arm is activated by pressing on body. Original. Marked "DLR 1966/3" on head and "Deluxe Reading Corp., N.J. 1966/2AB" on body. $20.00.

25" "Baby Heart Beat" with hard plastic head, glued-on wig, open mouth with two upper teeth. Cloth body with vinyl limbs. Has mechanism in body that when doll is tilted over and raised back up, the "heartbeat" can be heard. Made by and marked "DeSota." $45.00.

8" "Snoopy Astronaut." All vinyl and original. Marked "United Features Syn. Inc. 1969. Determined Productions, Inc." $22.00.

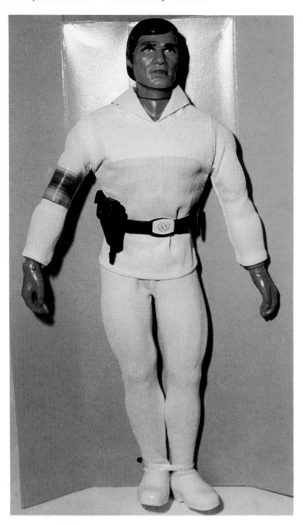

12½" "Buck Rogers" multi-jointed action figure made of plastic and vinyl. Has painted features and molded hair. Original. Marked "1979 Robert C. Dille." $38.00.

Walt Disney characters – 10" "Jiminy Cricket" and 12½" "Pinocchio." All composition and painted-on shoes. Both made by Knickerbocker Toy Co. Each - $350.00 up.

Walt Disney characters – 13" "Snow White" and 8" "Dwarfs." All composition with painted features and all original. Made by Knickerbocker. "Snow White" - $325.00 up; "Dwarfs" - $200.00 up each.

(For other Walt Disney characters, also see under Biken, Effanbee, and Tyco.)

Left: 8" "Pinocchio" made of plastic and vinyl. Unusual neck joint. Made for Walt Disney distributing Co. Molded-on hat marked "Walt Disney Prod." $10.00.

Right: 16" "Pinocchio" made of all wood. Cloth and felt clothes, molded-on cap. Made in Italy. $700.00.

Left: 22" "Mickey Mouse" made of soft plush and felt with felt pants and features. Tagged "Walt Disney Character manufactured by California Stuffed Toys." Late 1940s. $95.00.

Right: 18" "Mickey Mouse" is all plush with plastic eyes and felt mouth. Red pants sewn as part of figure. 1980s. $125.00.

6" "Mickey Mouse" bandmaster that is plastic and vinyl, fully jointed. Made in 1969–1970. $40.00.

10" "Donald Duck" and "Mickey Mouse" hand puppets. Vinyl with printed cloth mitt bodies. Marked "Walt Disney Productions. Made in Korea. 1978." Each - $12.00.

60th Anniversary musical "Mickey Mouse" and "Minnie Mouse" plush and cloth characters. Made by Applause, 1989. $50.00.

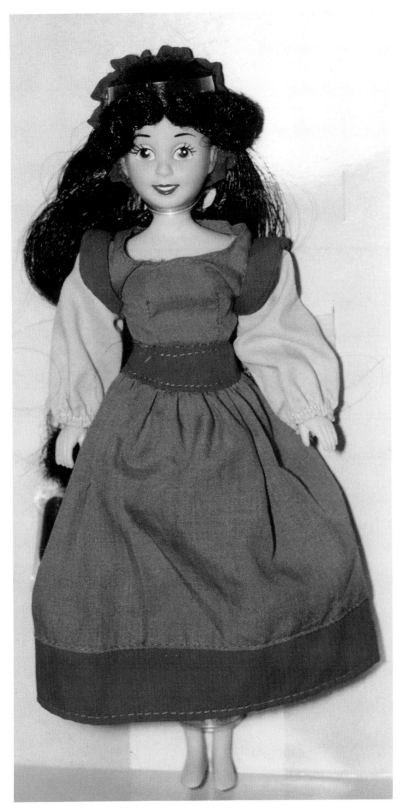

9½" "Snow White" is very pretty and made of plastic and vinyl with snapping knees and painted features. Information on box: "Filmation Presents Happy Ever After. Lucky Bell for Woolworth. 1990. Trademark of 1st National Film Corp. 1989. Made in China." $25.00.

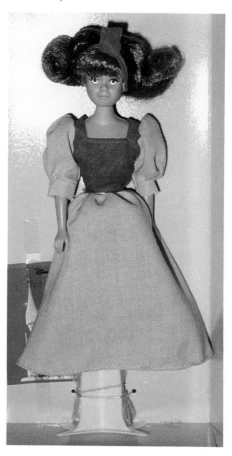

12" "Anastasia" (left) and "Drizella" (right) made of plastic and vinyl with painted features. Very round eyes with pupils looking upward. Characters are the wicked stepsisters from the Disney movie, *Cinderella*. Made by Bikin Express Ltd., 1988–1989. Each - $23.00.

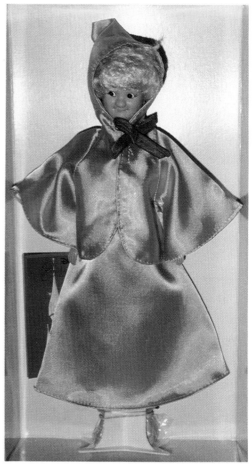

Above: 3" mice are flocked over vinyl with jointed necks, shoulders, and hips. From *Cinderella*. Made by Bikin Express Ltd. Set - $18.00. Right: 12" "Fairy Godmother" is made of plastic and vinyl with white rooted hair and smile mouth. Eyes painted to side. From *Cinderella*. Made by Bikin Express, Ltd., 1988–1989. $24.00.

12" "Cinderella" (left) and "Prince" (right) are plastic and vinyl with oval painted eyes. Made by Bikin Express Ltd., 1988–1989. Each - $35.00.

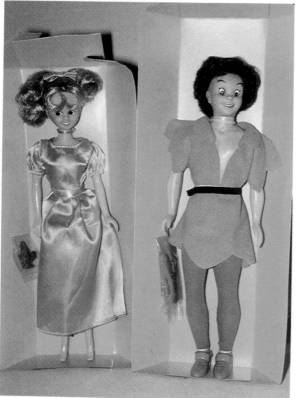

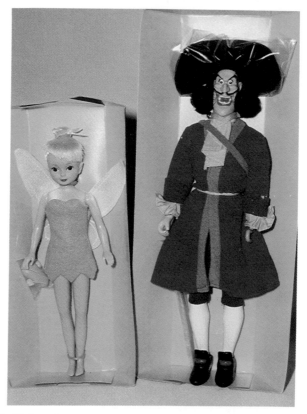

Left: 11" "Wendy" and 12" "Peter Pan." Right: 9" "Tinkerbelle" and 12" "Captain Hook." All are made of plastic and vinyl with painted features. "Captain Hook" has wide-open mouth, a gray hook, and painted-on white hoses. These Disney characters were made exclusively for Sears in 1987. Marked on heads "Made in China." Each - $35.00.

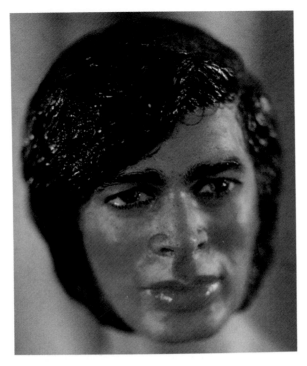

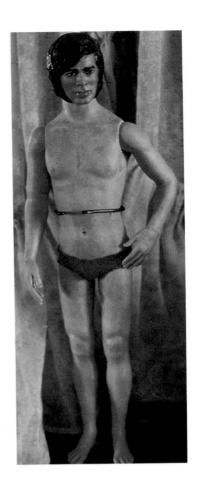

17" "Engelbert Humperdinck" made of all bisque with intaglio eyes, modeled hair and eyebrows. Made by N.I.A.D.A artist Pat Robinson in 1972. Above photo shows detail of face. Right photo shows complete body. $465.00 up.

Left: 20" "Patty O'Day" as portrayed by Jane Withers. Bisque and cloth, glass eyes, and open/closed mouth. Created by Judith Turner. $700.00 up.

Right: "Little Girl" is hand carved by Paul Spencer of Waco, Texas. Mr. Spencer carves dolls with sleep eyes and fully articulated bodies. He is one of the very few woodcarvers that leaves the wood in its natural state and stains some areas lightly. $465.00 up.

17" "Samantha" is all bisque with large glass eyes and sweet child's expression. Made by Lenox and limited to 750. Designer unknown. $1,200.00.

19" babies made of cloth and bisque. Weighted to feel lifelike. Head marked "Tyner Original/Boots Tyner 1987/ "Gumdrop" #1088." Clothes tagged "A Boots Tyner original." Each - $300.00.

20" "Sugar and Spice" (left) and "Everything Nice (right). Cloth and bisque with unusual jointed necks. Glass eyes. Designed and made for Kruger Dolls. Limited to 1,000 each. Each - $800.00.

Left: 13" "Ba, Ba, Black Sheep" with two bags of wool. 1989. Right: 13" beautiful child made in 1990. Both have glass eyes, bisque heads, and jointed bodies. Club Editions for Wendy Lawton Collector Guild. 1989 - $750.00; 1990 - $550.00.

13½" "The Little Angel" has vinyl baby body, real feather wings, and inset eyes. Designed by Lee Middleton for Kingdom Doll Co., Inc. in 1981. Limited edition of 1,000. Signed by Lee Middleton in black ink behind left ear under the hair. Head marked "10079-KDV 181/Little Angel/Lee Middleton 1979/Kingdom Doll Co./USA. $165.00.

20" "Lynne" has bisque head and hands with wood jointed body and glass eyes. Made by Roche in 1989. $800.00.

14" "Hansel & Gretel" is made of porcelain and cloth with glass eyes. Original. Made for Georgetown Collection by Abigail Brahms in 1987. Pair - $125.00.

18" "Easter Bunny" figures named "Rebecca" and "Calvin." Cloth body with wooden head, hands, and feet. Whiskers can fall out. These first series figures were designed and made by Raikis for Applause. Each - $200.00 up.

17" "Samatha" is a cloth/vinyl doll with sleep eyes. Excellent quality throughout. Made by Gotz for the Pleasant Hill Doll Co., 1988. $400.00.

21" child doll made of cloth and vinyl and has brown sleep eyes. Original. Made by Gotz in 1989. Marked "Gotz/ Puppen Germany." $225.00.

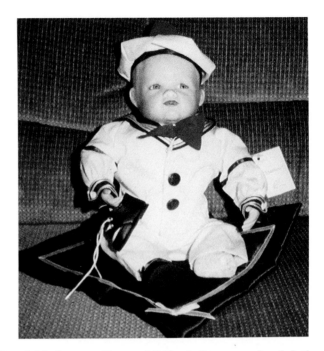

Left: 9½" "Amanda." Right: 10" "Matthew." Below: 10" "Sarah" in bunny slipper. All the dolls are made of cloth and bisque with inset eyes. These dolls are Knowles first series of "Picture Perfect Babies" and were marketed through The Ashton-Drake Galleries. Designed by Yolanda Bello in 1989. Each - $85.00.

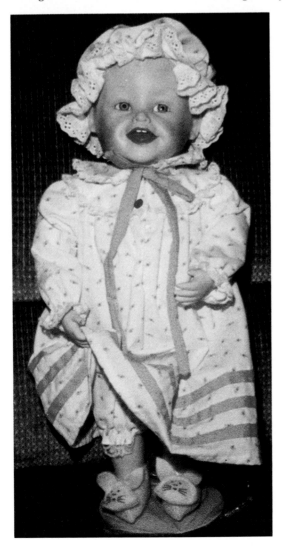

15½" "Melanie" is made of bisque and cloth with glass eyes. Regal Doll with a design copyright by Cardinal, Inc. and part of the Dynasty Collection. Made in 1988. $75.00.

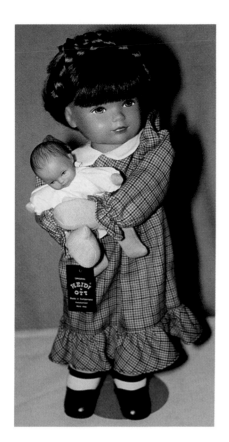

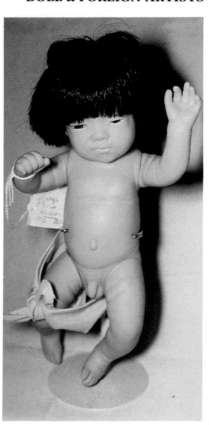

Left: 16" "Lucy & Her Baby" made of all cloth with vinyl heads. Marked "Heidi Ott 82-2-FAF. 1984." $225.00.

Right: 9" newborn is an all vinyl sexed boy doll with Asian features. Marked "Furga/Italy-1472" on head; "Furga, Italy 467" on back. 1983. $195.00.

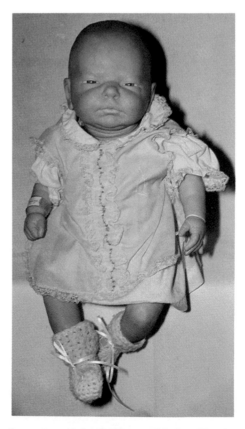

18" black newborn girl is all vinyl. Sexed and very life-like. Has pierced ears, inset eyes. Original. Marked "Furga" on head; "474/1988/Furga" on back. $175.00 up.

18" newborn is weighted like real baby. Has inset eyes, original. Made in Spain by Berjusa, 1980s. $155.00 up.

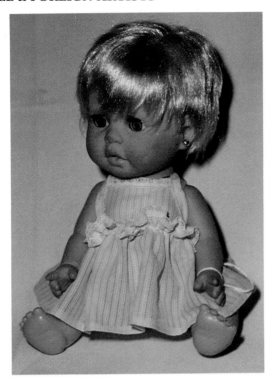

10" all vinyl doll with sleep eyes/lashes, pierced ears, and open/closed mouth. Made by Berjusa, Spain in early 1980s. $35.00.

19" "Joanie" made of all vinyl with set eyes. Original. Marked "Berjusa (Spain) 1988." $55.00.

21½" "Katja" doll is all original. Made by Zapf of Germany in 1985. $225.00.

21" "Exquisite" is cloth and vinyl with heavy rooted hair and pale sleep eyes. Original with knit sweater and leggings. Made by Zapf of Germany in 1982. $185.00.

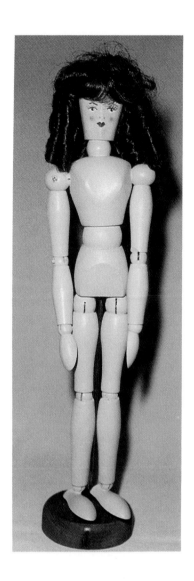

Above: 11" "Holly" girl and boy with painted features. Made by Silvestri. Each - $35.00.

Left: 12" all wood doll with body and limbs styled like antique dolls. Has metal joints and painted features. This unique original was created in 1991 by Kathy Tvrdik. $65.00.

Eegee/Goldberger Dolls

Dolls made by Eegee/Goldberger can be excellent or can be of rather "reasonable" quality. Goldberger is the actual company, but the product name came from the initials of the company founder's name – E.G. which became "Eegee."

As early as the 1930s, the excellent quality Eegee marked dolls were highly sought by collectors. Some of those dolls are "Miss Charming," an excellent quality Shirley Temple look-alike, and the 1951 "Gigi

Perreaux," the doll almost every personality collector would like to find. (This doll is shown on page 74 of *Modern Collector Dolls, Volume 1*.) It has an early vinyl head with laughing mouth on a hard plastic body.

Also "Flowerkins" are very collectible and are very hard to find in original outfits. They were made in 1963 and are marked "F/2" on their heads. The clothes are designed after flowers.

Left: 14" "Little Debutante Bride" made of vinyl and plastic with sleep eyes. Original. From 1958. Marked "Eegee" on head. $30.00.

Right: 15" all vinyl baby with inset eyes with lashes. Has open/closed mouth with molded tongue. First made in 1978, then again in 1986. Marked "Eegee" on head. Dolls marked "Made in China" are the 1986 dolls. $30.00.

Left: 20" plastic and vinyl doll with sleep eyes and upper and lower teeth. Lever on back of head makes mouth move. Marked "Eegee Co./2MM." $40.00.

Right: 26" "Lester" puppet is made of cloth and plastic. Original except for missing glasses. From 1976. $45.00.

30" "Grocho Marx" is cloth and rigid vinyl with molded hair. Pull string in back makes mouth move. First made in 1981. Marked "Eegee." $40.00.

27" "Charmer Bride" made of plastic and vinyl with long neck and delicate detailed hands. First made in 1961. Marked "15 BB/Eegee Co./1984/4." $65.00.

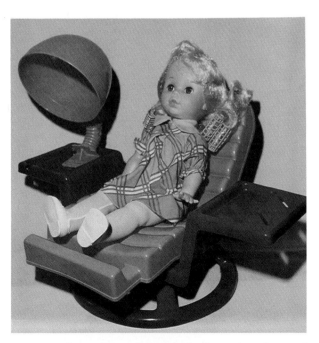

11½" "Diana" and 12" "Prince of Wales." Made by Launcy, Hachman & Harris and distributed by Goldberg (Eegee). 1983 – 1984. Set - $50.00.

17" "Sue and Her Beauty Salon." Black version also made. Marked "16 BP/Eegee Co." Box marked "Goldberger 1986." Complete set - $35.00; doll only - $18.00.

Left: 31" "Walking Annette." Made by Eegee, mid to late 1980s. Dress marked with doll's name and "•eg•" in black circle. Within circle is "A." $75.00.

Right: 11" "Howdy Doody" made of cloth and vinyl. Marked "Copyright 1972 National Broadcasting/Eegee Co/#3147/1987. $35.00.

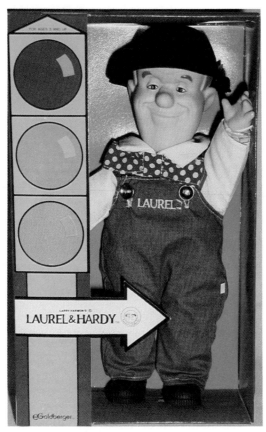

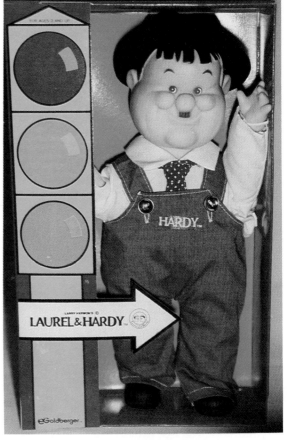

12" "Laurel" and "Hardy" are made of cloth and vinyl. Approved by Larry Harmon Picture Corp. Made in 1986. Marked "Eegee." Each - $25.00.

15" "Pouty Baby" made of cloth and vinyl with sleep eyes. Original. Marked "Eegee 1988." $50.00.

17" "Dolly Parton" is plastic and vinyl with painted features. Licensed exclusively by Eegee/Goldberger. Made in 1987 only. $75.00.

Effanbee Dolls

The "Patsy" family of dolls are the most widely collectible from this firm, but the rest of their dolls should not be overlooked, because the quality is excellent, and they are fun to collect.

In January 1992 the Alexander Doll Company purchased Effanbee and only the future will tell what will become of the doll line. Alexander would like to bring Effanbee back to the status of an important company and the 1993 doll line shows they will. The fact that "old" Effanbee dolls are not being made should not reduce their importance as collectibles. When found at shows, sales, and auctions, Effanbee dolls from 1970s – 1990s are selling at reasonable prices and should not be overlooked, especially if you like the "look" of the doll.

Right: 21" doll has open mouth, original floral print dress, and mohair wig. From 1925. Marked "Effanbee Rosemary/ Walk, Talk." $265.00.

Below: "Patsy" made of composition with cloth body and open mouth. This is the first original "Patsy." Shown in original clothes and has small Effanbee button. Made in 1924. $365.00.

19" "Patsy" as a nun (left) and child (center). Both are original except for replacement shoes on child. Both have molded hair and sleep eyes. Each - $475.00. 14" "Patsy" (right) is made of all composition with wig and sleep eyes. $365.00. All three dolls are ca. 1933.

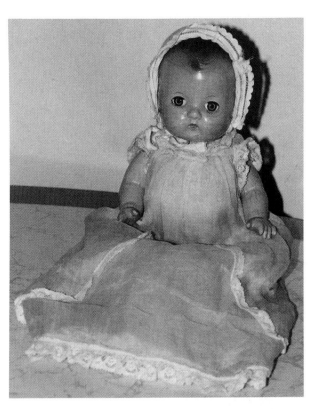

14" "Patsy" holding a tiny 9" "Wee Patsy" with painted-on shoes and socks. Both have painted features and are all original. 14" - $365.00; 9" - $345.00.

9" "Patsy Baby Babyette" made of all composition with unusual large sleep eyes. Original. $245.00.

14" Effanbee Historial Series dolls. Left: "Colonial Prosperity" for the year 1711. Right: "Later Carolina Settlement" for 1685. All composition with painted eyes. Original. Each - $600.00.

14" Effanbee Historial Series doll – "Louisana Purchase." Original with painted eyes. $600.00.

11" "Patsy Baby" made of all composition with sleep eyes. Magnetic hands hold various items. All original with original card that listed items hands would hold. Marked on head and body. Complete - $300.00.

9½" "George and Martha Washington" with mohair wigs, painted features, and all original. Both use "Patsyette" dolls. Each - $225.00.

21" "American Children" made of all composition with human hair wigs. Doll on left has sleep eyes; others have painted eyes. Original. Designed by Dewees Cochran in 1938. Each - $1,400.00.

14" "Skippy" is all composition with painted features. Original hat with pin. $465.00.

15" "Little Lady Majorette" is all composition with human hair wig and sleep eyes. All original. $350.00.

9" girl and boy "Patsyette Babies." All composition with sleep eyes and caracul wigs. All original clothes. Each - $265.00.

20" "Honey" is a beautiful doll made of all composition. Mint condition with original box. Ca. 1948–1949. Mint/boxed - $625.00; Played with - $400.00.

16" "Honey" made of all hard plastic. Original except for shoes. Marked "Effanbee. Made in U.S.A." $300.00. Shown with 14" "Toni" made of all hard plastic. Original. Made by Ideal Doll Co. $250.00.

20" "Dydee Baby" with hard plastic head that has a natural shine to it. Has rubber body and limbs and applied rubber ears. Original. $245.00.

11" "Portrait" doll. All compostition with sleep eyes. Original. $95.00 up.

16" "Honey" as "Prince Charming." All hard plastic. Replaced cap, cape, and wig. Marked "Effanbee" on head and "Effanbee/Made in U.S.A." on body. $400.00 up.

25" "Precious Baby" made of cloth and vinyl. First Limited Edition Club Doll in 1975. Head marked "Effanbee 1967." Dress tagged "Effanbee Limited Edition Doll." $550.00.

These are the Storyland Dolls made exclusively for Disney in 1977–1978. Left to right: "Sleeping Beauty," "Alice In Wonderland," "Cinderella," and "Snow White." Shown with the "Mary Poppins" set by Horsman. Effanbee only - $250.00 each.

Above: Dolls from the Grand Dames Series in 1980 – 15"
"Jezebel" (left) and 18" "Coco" (right). Both have excellent
quality clothes. (Before 1980, "Jezebel" was "Civil War
Lady" in the Passing Parade Series.) Each - $75.00.

Left: 18" "Bride" has the "pinched" Nicole face. From
the 1980 Bridal Suite Collection. $80.00.

Left: 17" "Groucho Marx" has modeled-on glasses. Marked "Effanbee/1983" on head. Right: 16" "James Cagney" from 1987. Dolls from Effanbee's Legend Series. Each - $45.00.

Others in the series are W.C. Fields (1980), John Wayne (1982), John Wayne and Mae West (1983), Judy Garland/ Dorothy of Oz (1985), Lucille Ball (1986).

Below: 15" "Winston Churchill." All original. From Great Moments In History Collection, 1984. $45.00.

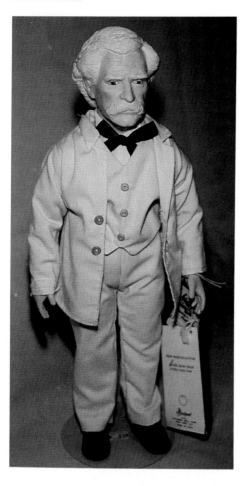

Left: 16" "Mark Twain" with white modeled hair and mustache. Right: 13" "Huck Finn" with leg modeled bent. Both are from the Mark Twain Collection and are made of plastic and vinyl. Marked "Effanbee/1983." Each - $40.00.

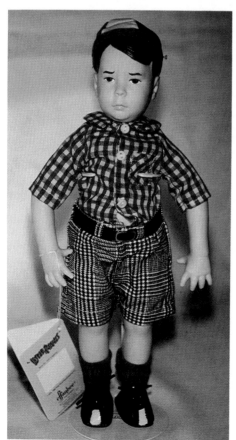

Left: 11½" "Spanky" with painted features, "tough kid" expression, and molded hair. Marked "King World." Right: 11" "Buckwheat" with rooted hair, painted features, and wide smile. Both are from the Little Rascal Collection. Original, 1989. Each - $35.00.

Left: 14" "Isabella Of Spain." Original with rooted hair. Right: 16" "King Ferdinand" with molded hair. Below: 16" "Columbus." Original with molded hair. New World Collection from 1989. Each - $85.00.

Left: 17" "Thomas Jeffereson" with molded hair and painted features. Original, 1989. $45.00. Right: 16" "Harry Truman" with molded hair under hat. Original, 1988. $45.00. Below: 16" "Dwight D. Eisenhower" with molded hair under cap. Original, 1987. Dolls are from Effanbee's The Presidents Series. $50.00.

9½" "Baby Liza" made of all vinyl with one leg bent. Bow glued to top of head. Original. From 1980. $30.00.

11½" "Queen of Hearts" storybook doll. Plastic and vinyl with sleep eyes. All original. From 1985. $35.00.

11½" "Mother Goose" made of plastic and vinyl with sleep eyes. Original, 1984 – 1987. $35.00.

"Little Old New York" dolls made of plastic and vinyl with very sweet faces, painted features, and dressed in sailor suits. Made in 1987. Each - $40.00.

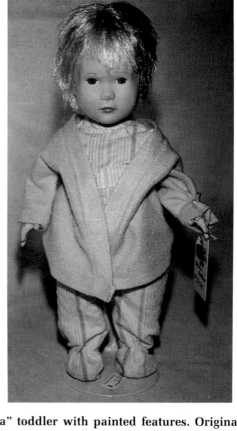

11½" "Kim" made of plastic and vinyl with painted features. Original. From One World Collection. 1980. $45.00.

9" "Lisa" toddler with painted features. Original. From 1980. $30.00.

11½" "Hansel and Gretel." Both dolls original. From Storybook Collection of 1984 – 1986. $30.00.

11½" doll from Christmas Together Collection. Original. From mid-1980s. $35.00.

11" "Friday" made of plastic and vinyl with sleep eyes. Original. From the Day By Day Collection of 1980. Marked "Effanbee" on head and body. $45.00.

14" "Patsy" made of all vinyl with painted hair and features. Original in tan coat and cap with red scarf and gloves. From 1987. $48.00.

This 8" doll came in many different outfits. Has rooted hair and sleep eyes. From the Lil' Innocents Collection of late 1980s. $28.00.

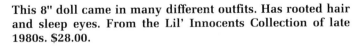

Left: 12" "The Wrangler" wears authorized Wrangler jeans, vest, and shirt. Plastic and vinyl with painted features. Has molded hair and mustache. Made by Ertl in 1982. $105.00. Right: 11½" "Missy" also wears Wrangler jeans and jacket. Plastic and vinyl with painted features. Made by Ertl in 1982. $95.00.

16" "Old Fashioned Girl" has vinyl head, legs, and lower arms. Rest is cloth. Painted features and marked "1986 Eugene Doll Co." $30.00.

12" "Happy Birthday Baby" made of cloth and vinyl with sleep eyes and lashes. Marked "1987 Eugene Doll & Novelty Co." $20.00.

13" "My Baby" made of cloth and vinyl with sleep eyes and lashes. Original. Marked "1987 Eugene Doll Co." $18.00.

18" "Suzie Sez" is made of cloth with gautlet vinyl hands. Vinyl head with puppet mouth. Pull string in back. Original. Head marked "Eugene 8 M 10. 1987." $35.00.

13" "Ballerina" is plastic and vinyl with sleep eyes. Original. Marked "Eugene 1987." $24.00.

18" "Satin 'N Lace" made of cloth and vinyl with open/closed mouth, two upper teeth, sleep eyes. Original. Marked "Eugene 1987." $22.00.

14" black "Satin 'N Lace" made of cloth and vinyl with sleep eyes. Marked "1987 Eugene Doll Co." on head. Original. $22.00.

13" "Su Ling" made of plastic and vinyl. From the My Best Friend set. Made by Eugene Co. in 1987. Marked "Made in U.S.A. 1987" on head. $30.00.

11" military dolls from Desert Shield set. Left: "Navy Seal." Right: "Scout." Made in China for Eugene Co. in 1990. Each - $28.00.

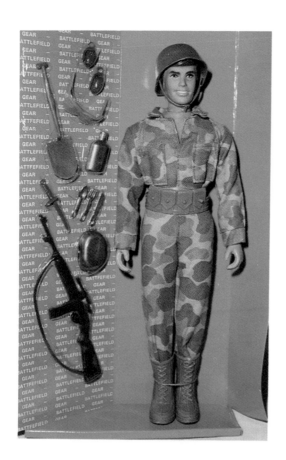

11" military dolls from Desert Shield set. Top left : "Trooper." Top right: "Gunner." Bottom left: "Paratrooper." Bottom right: "Sergent." Made in China for Eugene Doll Co. in 1990. Each - $28.00.

30" "Billie Peppers Old Friends" railroad man. Cloth with ceramic gauntlet hands and head. Painted features. Original. Designed by Billie Peppers of Boaz, Alabama. Made in China by Fibre-Craft Material Corp. in 1987. Marked "Copyright Billie Peppers 1986." $285.00.

10½" "Showgirl" souvenir doll with painted features and applied glitter outfit and accessories. Made by Fiona Original of Las Vegas, 1979. Tagged "Made in Las Vegas." $22.00.

Fisher-Price

CHRONOLOGICAL LISTING
(Courtesy of Carla Connell)

1974: The six soft girls, #200 – 505

1975: Joey in the soft series, #206

1976: Honey, soft print body, #208

1977: My Friend Mandy, first issue, #210
Mandy clothes, outfits #215 – 218

1978: My Baby Beth, #209
Mandy clothes, outfits #219 – 222

1979: My Friend Mandy, second issue, #211
My Friend Jenny, first issue, #212
My Friend clothes, outfits #223 – 225,
shoes/tights #226

Four Seasons Fashions patterns/story, #235
My Sleepy Baby, #207
Fisher-Price Kids, four soft-body dolls,
#240 – 243

1980: Baby Soft Sounds (makes cooing sounds),
#213
Baby Soft Sounds, Black, #214
Bundle-Up Baby in bassinet, #244
My Friend clothes, outfits #288 – 229

1981: Henson Muppet Toys, Kermit, #857
Kermit clothes, sleepwear #889
Henson Muppet Toys, Miss Piggy, #890
Miss Piggy clothes, outfits #891 – 893

Baby Ann and Her Care Set, #249
Bobbie, soft doll, #245
My Friend clothes, outfits #230 – 231
1982: Henson Muppet Toys, The Great Gonzo,
#858
Kermit/Gonzo clothes (interchangeable),
outfit #887 – 888
Miss Piggy clothes, outfit #889
My Friend Mandy, third issue, #215
My Friend Jenny, second issue, #217
My Friend Becky, only issue, #218
My Friend Mikey, only issue, #205
My Friend clothes, outfits #232 – 233
Susie Soft Sounds (has sleep eyes), #201
(reused 1974 Jenny number)
Baby/Susie Soft Sounds clothes,
outfits #294 – 296
1983: Henson Muppets Kermit The Frog, #850
Henson Muppets Kermit The Frog hand
puppet, #860
Henson Beanbag Muppets Assort
(Miss Piggy, Kermit, Gonzo, Fozzie) #899
Forget-Me-Not Babies Posie, #202;
Rosie, #203; Honey, #204
1984: My Friend Mandy, fourth issue (new face),
#216
My Friend Jenny, third issue (longer hair),
#209 (reused Baby Beth number)
My Friend Nicky (Black girl), #206 (reused
Joey's 1975 number)
1985: My Bathing Baby, #241 (Reused Fisher-
Price Kids Muffie's number)
My Comb & Care Baby, #242 (Reused
Fisher-Price Kids Billie's number)
My Very First Baby, #243 (Reused
Fisher-Price Kids Bobbie's number)
Special Birthday Mandy, #4009
My Little Sister Mary (uncataloged), #200
(Reused 1974 Mary's number)
(Note: Face is Mandy, Issues 1 – 3)
My Friend clothes sold separately, i.e.:
#238 is Mandy #3 issue dress,
#4108 is Becky's dress. (Issue number not
available.)
#4109 is Mandy #4 issue outfit,
#4110 is Jenny #3 issue outfit
1986: No new issues shown, only continuation
appears to be #241 – 243 from 1985
1991: New My Friend Dolls,
#8123 Christie in two different dress;
#8121 Karen (black doll);
#8122 Megan (1974 body design)
Puffalump Kids –
#4091 Sherri; #4092 Merri; #4094
Heidi; #4094 Whitney (black);
#4096 Greg

12" "Baby's First Doll" has pink and white check non-removable clothes and tuff of yarn hair. Design much like Madame Alexander's "Funny." This is a baby item and is #120. It has been on the market since 1975. $50.00.

12" "Honey" with cloth body and limbs with vinyl gauntlet hands and head with molded hair. Body tagged "Fisher-Price Toys/East Aurora, N.Y./1975." $40.00.

16" "My Friend Mandy" in extra boxed outfit. Has pink rose print on white cloth body. Vinyl head and painted features. Marked "43/20141/1976/ Fisher-Price" on head and has body tag. First issue: #210, 1976/1977. Pink dress with white dots. $65.00. Second issue: #211, 1979. Floral stripe dress. $45.00. Third issue: #215, 1982. Navy dress with white dots. $35.00.

17" "My Baby Beth" with foam-filled body, vinyl head and limbs, rooted hair, and painted features. Has body tag. Marked "47/21200/1977/Fisher-Price Toys" on head. $35.00.

8" "Fisher-Price Kids" with vinyl heads and cloth bodies. Removable hat, shirt, or jacket. Left to right: "Mikey" marked "4/225801/Fisher-Price Toys/1978." Body tagged: "#240." "Muffy" marked "52/225371/Fisher-Price Toys/1978." Body tagged: "#241." "Bobbie" marked "0/22587/Fisher-Price Toys/1978." Body tagged: "#243." (Not pictured is "Billie.") Each - $28.00.

18" "Kermit The Frog" made of all green felt with white plastic eyes. Box marked "A Jim Henson Muppet Doll 850/ Kermit The Frog/Fisher-Price Toys/850 Assembled in Mexcio/Henson Associates Inc. 1956, 1976/Fisher-Price 1976/1977." Body tag has same information. $28.00.

6½" "Miss Piggy" has vinyl head with bean bag style body. Marked "Fisher-Price Toys/Division of the Quaker Oats Co./867/Assembled in Mexico/Miss Piggy/A Jim Henson Muppet Doll." 14" "Miss Piggy" with flesh-colored body. Additional outfits were available. Marked "1980 Henson Assoc./2978G" and body tag marked same as small doll. 6½" – $14.00; 14" - $20.00.

16" "My Friend Jenny" with vinyl head and limbs with yellow rose print on white cloth body. Red hat and shoes not original. Marked "9/83088/Fisher-Price Toys/1978." Has body tag. $65.00. Shown with second issue doll that is marked same except body tagged "1982/217." $45.00.

19" "My Sleepy Baby" with cloth body and limbs and vinyl gauntlet hands and head. Sleep eyes, rooted hair. Marked "2/Fisher-Price Toys/1978/22689." Body tagged "Fisher-Price Toys/1978/207/Assembled in Mexico from U.S. and foreign components." $42.00.

16" "Baby Soft Sounds" has cloth body with vinyl head and limbs, rooted hair, and painted features. Body has sewn-on underwear. Zippered opening across bottom for battery-operated voice box. Marked "52/27351/Fisher-Price Toys/1979." Body tagged "#213." $38.00.

12" "Baby Ann" made of cloth and vinyl with painted features. Marked "4398/8/2805G/Fisher-Price Toys/1980" on head. Body tagged "#249." $27.00.

13" "Bobbie" has cloth body and limbs, sewn-on bonnet, and vinyl face with painted features and orange hair. Tagged "Fisher-Price Toys/Division of the Quaker Oats Co./1980. #245." $28.00.

17" "Susie Soft Sounds" made of cloth and vinyl with sleep eyes. Battery operated, cries and stops when picked up or put on stomach. Marked "33928/Fisher-Price Toys/1981." $30.00.

16" "My Friend Mikey" made of cloth and vinyl. Marked "21/33067/Fisher-Price Toys/1981." Body tagged "#205." $30.00.

6" "Rosie" made of vinyl with terry cloth body and limbs. Came with cap and matching blanket. One of the "Forget-Me-Not Babies." Marked "0-225381/Fisher-Price Toys/1978." Body tagged "1982 #202, 203, 204." $12.00.

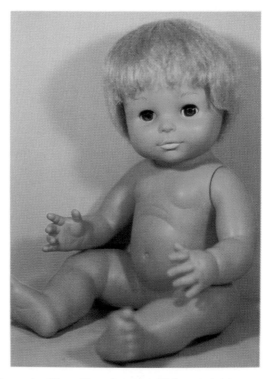

14½" "My Bathing Baby" is all vinyl with sleep eyes. Marked "4618/14/Hong Kong/379881/Fisher-Price/1982" on head. Body detail is shown on nude doll at right. $30.00.

16" "My Friend Becky" with red hair and freckles. In extra boxed outfit. (Brunette is "Jenny"; blonde is "Mandy.") Marked "18/33340/Fisher-Price Toys/1983." $40.00.

15" "My Care & Comb Baby" with rose print on white cotton body. Vinyl head and limbs. Rooted hair, sleep eyes. Original overalls, replaced blouse. Marked "4726/A2862T/ Fisher-Price Toys/1984." Body tagged "#242." $38.00.

14" "My Little Sister Mary" with vinyl head, cloth body, and painted features. Permanent outfit with removable blue skirt (missing). Marked "53/20141/1976/Fisher-Price Toys." Body tagged "#200, 1984." $28.00.

15" "My Very First Baby" with rose print on white cotton body, sleep eyes, and vinyl head and hands. White silky sock feet/booties. Original jumper dress. Has slight smile with dimples. Marked "39280/Fisher-Price Toys/1982." Body tagged "1984, #243." $40.00.

Left: 16" "Special Birthday Mandy" has yellow rose print on white cloth body, vinyl head and limbs, and painted features. Original. This is the fifth and last issue of Mandy. Marked "18/39608L/1983/Fisher-Price Toys." Body tag includes the copyright dates of #216 – 1982; #209 – 1984; #218 – 1981 and this issue #4009 – 1985. $55.00.

Right: 16" "My Friend Becky" has yellow rose print on white cloth body with vinyl head and limbs. Marked "4/35540/Fisher-Price Toys/1987." Body tagged "1984, #218." $42.00.

Above: 14" "My Friend Christie" #8120 (left) and "My Friend Karen #8121 (right). Vinyl heads and hands. Cloth body dressed in non-removable basic outfit with removable dress. Only 200 "Karen" dolls were available. Marked "78368/Fisher-Price Toys/1990." "Christie" - $35.00; "Karen" - $40.00.

Left: 17" "Baby Ann" made of cloth and vinyl. This dolls in from 1983. Marketed in 1980. Marked "87/87351/ Fisher-Price Toys/1979." $45.00.

15" "Baby Smiles" has a stockinette body and limbs with vinyl head. Heart-shaped painted pupils. Original. Marked "88 Fleetwood Toy Inc. Made in China." $28.00.

Franklin Mint

The "lady" or "fashion" dolls from the Franklin Mint are some of the *best* quality dolls being offered by all the mints, galleries, and such. The quality of artist painting is excellent, and the workmanship and design of the clothes could hardly be improved. These "ladies" and their costumes do take up room due to their size, but the quality is worth it. The future looks bright for all these fine dolls.

"Snow White" in the Disney Crest Colors. Cloth and bisque. Holds a bisque apple in hand. Finest quality for artist doll. Issued by Franklin Mint. $275.00 up.

20" "Gibson Bride" has cloth body and bisque head/limbs. Painted features, excellent quality. Issued by Franklin Mint. $300.00 up.

21" "Rose Princess" made of porcelain and cloth. Winner of the 1990 Award of Excellence by Doll of the Year voting. (Detail of doll is shown in above photo.) $200.00 up.

109

"Cinderella" is made of porcelain and cloth. Wears beautiful mauve gown and hand spun glass slipper. Designed for Franklin Mint by Gerda Neubacher in 1989. $285.00 up.

Close-up of "Cinderella." Note excellent detail of the face and hair. Wears exquisite rhinestone and cultured pearl jewelry.

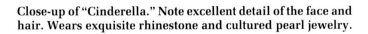

6½" cats are made of porcelain and cloth with painted-on shoes. Delightfully dressed in removable clothes. Each has a personality of its own. Made for the Franklin Mint. Each - $30.00.

"Morton Salt Girl" is made of cloth and bisque with painted features, hair, and footwear. From the Franklin Mint Country Store Collection. $65.00.

Fisk Tire Doll with cloth body and bisque head, limbs, and tire. Made by Franklin Mint. $65.00.

Dolls from Franklin Mint's Country Store Collection. Top row: "Dutch Boy Paint Boy," "Mary Jane Candy Girl," Bottom row: "Ceresota Flour Boy," "J.P. Coats Thread Girl." Made of cloth and bisque. Each - $65.00.

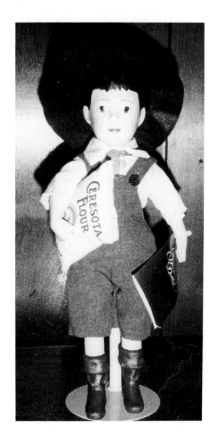

12" "Lone Ranger" and horse "Silver." Multi-jointed plastic and original. Marked "Gabriel/1974." Set - $95.00.

12" "Tonto" and horse "Scout." Multi-jointed plastic and original. Marked "Gabriel/1974." Set - $100.00.

Multi-jointed action figures made by Gabriel. "Dan Reed" with horse "Banjo" set - $45.00. Shown with "Red Sleeves" and "Little Bear" set - $60.00.

Above: 1½" & 2" "Sweet Secrets" jewelry that makes into a doll. Marked "1984-1985/Galoob Inc. U.S.A." Patented, with some marked "Pat. Pending." Each - $14.00.

Left: 13" "Pretty Cut & Grow." Vinyl with painted features. Yarn hair comes with extra yarn hair plus styling booklet, scissors, comb, ribbons, and barrettes. Marked "Gabriel/1980. CBS Inc. Lancaster, PA 17602/Made in U.S.A./Pat. Pend." on back. $32.00.

12" "Mr. T" from the "A-Team" television show. Plastic and vinyl, all original. Holes in hands for tools and weapons. Made by Galoob in 1983. $28.00.

12" "Talking Mr. T" is made of plastic and vinyl. Hands molded to hold tools. Marked "1983 Stephen J. Cannell Production. Made by Galoob." $38.00.

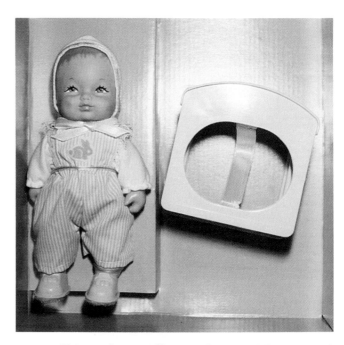

Necklace that makes into a bear. All parts fold inside. Made by Galoob in 1984. $14.00.

6½" "Walking Baby & Walker" with painted features and hair. Battery operated. Made by Galoob in 1988. $30.00.

Left: 20" "Baby Talk" made of cloth and vinyl with sleep eyes. Battery operated. Original. Marked "1985/Galoob Inc." $36.00. Right: 18" "Punky Brewster" from NBC television show by same name. Made of plastic and vinyl with freckles. Original. Head marked "Galoob/ 1984/N.B.C., Inc./Made in China." $38.00.

8" "Bouncin' Ballerina Kid" made of vinyl and plastic with plastic crown. Multi-position knee joints. Jointed in middle of one foot. Marked "1988 L.G.T.I." on head. Tagged "1989 Lewis Galoob Toys/Made in China." $29.00.

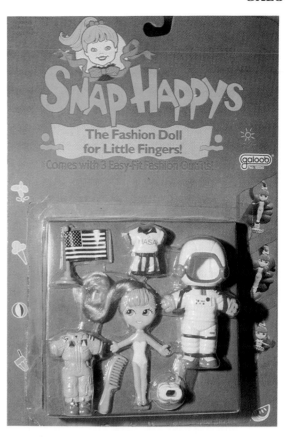

3" "Snap Happy" set called "Out in Space." Doll is flat with painted features. Molded hair with rooted ponytail. Made in China by Galoob in 1989. $18.00.

8" "Bouncin' Princess" with magic light-up tiara. Battery operated. Marked "1989/Galoob." $20.00.

17½" "So Funny Natalie" is all vinyl and plastic with jointed knees. Wide open mouth, inset eyes, and original. From Baby Face Collection. Marked "Galoob/1990." $38.00.

17½" "So Innocent Cynthia" with large round inset eyes. Plastic and vinyl with jointed knees. From Baby Face Collection. Marked "Galoob/1990." $38.00.

13" "So Playful Penny" with inset eyes, jointed elbows and knees, and wide open mouth. Made by Galoob. Marked "1990 G.T.I./#10 China." $38.00.

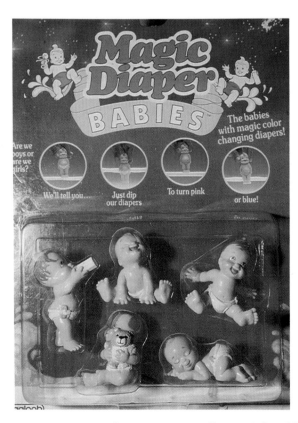

2½" "Magic Diaper Babies." Diapers will turn pink or blue when placed in water. Made by Galoob, 1991. $10.00.

27" "Susie Scribble." She writes and draws – an amazing battery-operated doll. Original. Created by Wonderama Toys, Inc. and marked "H. Garfinkle." $200.00.

16" "Gerber Baby" made of cloth with all vinyl arms and heads. Sleep eyes that are not flirty. Molded hair. Original. Marked "1989 Gerber Prod. Co./All Rights Reserved." $28.00.

10" and 6" "Gerber Babies." Heads marked "1988 Gerber Products." Tagged "1989 Made by Lucky Industries." 10" - $20.00; 6" - $12.00.

Gorham

It is difficult to understand why certain Gorham made dolls are priced as high as they are. Most were reproductions with high colored bisque and poor quality clothes. Later they seemed to change to a little better quality painting and perhaps the "limited edition" idea is what makes some so "sought after." For example, some dolls that were sold for $150.00 are now being offered for $500.00. At the same time, there are many Gorham dolls on the *first* market (retail) priced from $125.00 to as high as $700.00, because they are limited editions.

"Clementine" has cloth body, upper arms, and upper legs. The rest is bisque. In original costume. This doll is the 100th anniversary edition made exclusively for Belk & Leggett. From the Southern Heritage Collection by Gorham. Wind-up music box plays "Oh, My Clementine." Each doll is numbered. Only 800 were made. Made in 1988. $400.00.

11½" "Candy Girl" made of plastic and vinyl with jointed waist, painted features, and rooted hair. Made by Hamilton Toys, Inc., 1990. $30.00.

8" "Fred Flintstone" and 3½" "Dino" are all vinyl with jointed neck and shoulders. Fred is marked "Trademark of Screen Gems/Hanna-Barbera Productions, Inc. 1970." Dino is marked "1988 Hanna-Barbera Productions." Fred Flintstone - $12.00; Dino - $8.00.

12" "G.I. Joe Frogman" is multi-jointed. Made by Hasbro in 1964. $90.00 up.

14" "Bathing Beauty" made of vinyl and plastic with large, round painted eyes and open/closed mouth. Original with terry cloth towel. Marked "Hasbro Corp. 1972." $30.00.

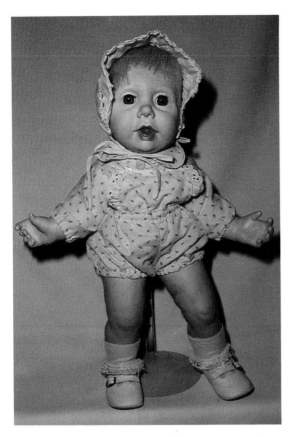 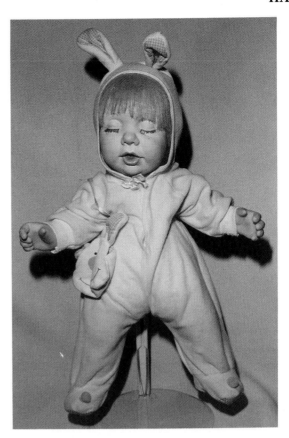

Left: 20" "Real Baby" with inset eyes and lashes. Right: 20" "Sleeping Real Baby" in original bunny suit. Both are made of cloth with soft vinyl arms and legs and rigid vinyl head. Dolls are weighted like newborn baby. Marked "1984 J. Turner/Hasbro. Made in Hong Kong." Each - $40.00.

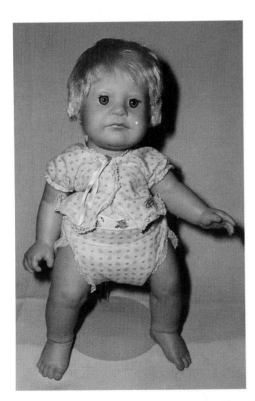 

18" "Real Baby" with weighted cloth body and vinyl head and limbs. Inset eyes with lashes. Marked "J. Turner/1985/ Hasbro Inc." $35.00.

24" "My Buddy" with cloth body and limbs. Hands with stitched fingers. Vinyl head with painted features and freckles. Made by Hasbro in 1985. $35.00.

5½" Moon Dreamer dolls. "Sparky Dreamer" (left) with plastic star-shaped glasses and yellow hair. "Sparky Dreamer" (right) with pink hair. Purple painted eyes; star painted around one eye. (Other dolls in the set are "Crystal Dreamer" with pink hair, "Dream Gazer" with orange hair and sparkle, "Whimzie" with blue hair, and boy doll, "Buck.") Marked "1986 Hasbro/Made in Korea." Each - $15.00.

Dolls from the "Jem" set. Left: 12" "Kimber" with bright orange hair and blue eyes. Jointed wrists and waist. Center: 12" "Stomer" of the "Misfits." Blue curly hair; blue eyes with yellow eyeshadow. Right: 12" with dark purple hair, blue eyes with yellow eyeshadow around one eye, blue around the other. Made by Hasbro in 1986. Each - $35.00.

From the Jem and The Holograms collection. Left: 12" doll with pink hair, pink and blue eyeshadow, and bright pink lips. Center: 12" "Shanna" of the Jem's Hologram backup band. Pale lavender curly hair, brown eyes outlined in white. Jointed waist and wrists. Right: 12" "Aja" from Jem's backup band. Blue hair, gray eyes, and blue star on cheek. Jointed wrists and waists. Made by Hasbro in 1986. Each - $35.00.

Left: 12" "Jem Rock Star" who becomes "Jemica," owner of Starlight Music. White hair with lavender eyes. Hasbro, 1986. Center: Entire 12" doll is lavender in color. Purple hair and green eyes. Right: 12" doll with pink, blue, and blonde hair. Bright blue eyes. One of "Jem" set. Jointed waist and wrist. All dolls made by Hasbro in 1986. Each - $35.00.

Left: 12" doll which is one of the "Jem" group. Pink hair in back; blonde with gold threads in front. Lavender eyes, jointed wrists and waist. Hasbro, 1986. $40.00. Center: 12" "Roxy of the Misfits." White hair, brown painted eyes, light green "wing" eye outline. Jointed wrists and waist. $35.00. Right: 12" "Stormer of the Misfits" from the "Jem" set. Yellow hair, lavender eyeshadow. Jointed waist and wrists. Made by Hasbro in 1986. $40.00.

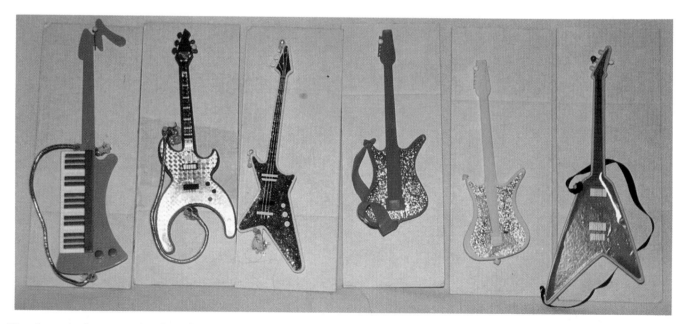

"Jem" musical accessories from left to right: Keyboard belongs to "Knicker" of the Holograms. Silver guitar belongs to "Pizazz" of the Misfits. Blue guitar belongs to "Aja." Bright pink guitar to "Shanna" of the Holograms. The yellow is one of "Jem's" guitars. The purple guitar belongs to "Kimber." Each - $40.00 up.

Left: 12" "Jem" with blonde hair that flows to pink. Has bend knees. Made by Hasbro. $35.00.

Right: 12½" "Rio" who is Jem's road manager and Jemica's boyfriend. Jointed waist, bend knees, and jointed wrists. Hasbro, 1986. $40.00.

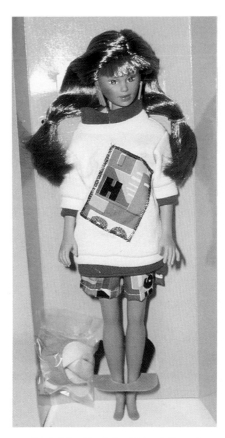

11½" "Dance 'n Romance Maxie" has blonde hair and blue eyes. Grow hair feature. Made by Hasbro in 1987. $30.00.

11½" "Ashley" of the "Maxie" set has bendable knees and red hair. Made by Hasbro in 1987. $25.00.

Left: 11½" "Kristen" of the "Maxie" set. Black hair, brown eyes, and bendable knees. Hasbro, 1987. $25.00.

Right: 11½" "Carly" of the "Maxie" set. Dark blonde hair, lavender eyes with blue/lavender eyeshadow. Bendable knees. Marked 1987/ Hasbro." $25.00.

8" with pale yellow hair and green/gold eyes. Blue vinyl molded-on undies and socks. Marked "1987 Hasbro/All Rights Reserved." $18.00.

16" oriental Cabbage Patch on rocking horse. Marked "Hasbro 1989." $40.00.

16" Designer Cabbage Patch in car. Has flat top hairdo with very dark red hair. Marked "Hasbro 1989." Complete - $50.00.

17½" "Marissa" made of plastic and vinyl with painted features. Brunette with blue eyes. From the "My Beautiful Doll" set. Marked "1989 Hasbro." $30.00.

17½" "Brenda." made of plastic and vinyl with painted features and blue eyes. Blonde hair with plastic tiara. From "My Beautiful Doll" set. Marked "1989 Hasbro." $45.00.

12" "Duke - Hall of Fame G.I. Joe." Outfitted in Desert Storm fatigues. Very limited edition, sold through Target Stores in 1991. Made by Hasbro. $95.00.

127

23" "Laurel & Hardy" made of cloth and plastic with pull string to operate mouth. Made in 1984. Marked "Larry Harmon H-24." Each - $25.00.

13" "Rock 'n Dance" made of vinyl and plastic with plastic feet/shoes. Battery operated. Made by Hip Yick International in 1986. Marked "Made in Taiwan/Pat. Pend. Taiwan and U.S.A." $22.00.

11½" "Vanna White" from TV show "Wheel of Fortune." Had 12 different outfits available. Purchased only through cable TV's Home Shopping Club. The first ones were in limited editions. Marked "H.S.C. 1990." $28.00.

Left: 15" "Paula" Cloth and bisque with green glass eyes. Made by Seymore Mann. Limited to 2,500 and sold through cable TV's Home Shopping Club. Marked "Copyright Mann '89." Has maple leaf decal with "mann" across the middle and "MCMLXXVII." $45.00. Right: 16" "Linda" has freckles and blue glass eyes. Made by Seymore Mann. Sold through Home Shopping Club. Marked same as other doll. $40.00.

Horsman Doll Company

Horsman dolls have always interested collectors, because over the years they made some very unique dolls. They are known for the "He-Bee, She-Bee" dolls, "Ella Cinder," and the "Campbell Kids" as well as many other characters from the early years. In the 1930s the company produced composition dolls of the highest quality. When the company moved into the hard plastic and plastic and vinyl eras, the tradition of excellence continued in their dolls.

The "Patsy" style dolls from Horsman was marketed under two names – "Dorothy" and "Sally." Hard plastic dolls marked "170" are also Horsman creations.

During the 1950s – 1970s, Horsman dolls bore a "family" resemblance. Irene Szor designed dolls for the company at that time, and her style is very apparent in all the dolls she made. These dolls from this time period will be marked with Szor's name on the doll or the box.

Collectors, if you see a Horsman doll you like, do not overlook it. If the price is right, buy and enjoy it.

Left: 10½" "He-Bee" is all composition with painted features. Jointed at shoulders and hips. Has molded-on teddy and booties. 1925. $525.00 up.

Right: 19" toddler made of cloth and composition with tin sleep eyes. Open mouth with dimples. Marked "E.I.H. Co. Inc." (E.I. Horsman). Ca. 1933. $225.00. Shown with 14" "Baby Dainty" made of cloth and composition. Outfited in tagged dress. Made by Effanbee. Marked with name. $165.00.

Above: 22" "Chubby Baby" made of cloth with composition head and limbs. Sleep, flirty eyes, molded hair. Ca. 1946. Marked "Horsman." $125.00.

Left: 19" "Bright Star Majorette" made of all composition with open mouth and sleep eyes. Second and third fingers molded together. Right arm molded slightly bent. Ca. 1937. Marked "Horsman." $385.00.

10" "Ballerina" made of vinyl and rigid vinyl. Has jointed knees, ankles, and waist. Gold tutu, replaced slippers. From 1958. Marked "Horsman" on head. $35.00.

15" "Hansel & Gretel" made of all soft vinyl with rooted hair implanted into scalp. Sleep eyes. Original. From 1963. Dolls are unmarked but tagged "Horsman Doll Co." Each - $245.00.

10½" "Christopher Robin" and 3" "Winnie The Pooh" in original box. He is plastic and vinyl with rooted hair, painted features and marked "Horsman Doll, Inc." "Pooh" is marked "1964 Disney Prod." Set - $50.00.

12" "Mary Poppins" with "Michael" and "Jane" in original box. All are plastic and vinyl. From 1960s. Marked "Horsman Dolls." Set in box - $165.00.

Left: 17" "Cindy" made of vinyl and rigid vinyl with sleep eyes. High heel feet shown with replaced shoes. (Doll looks very much like "Cissy" from Madame Alexander.) Made in early 1960s. Marked "Horsman." $65.00 up.

Right: 9" "Angie Dickenson – Policewoman." Jointed waist, posable limbs, painted features. Original but missing shoes. Marked "Horsman Dolls Inc./U/L/8 1976." $20.00.

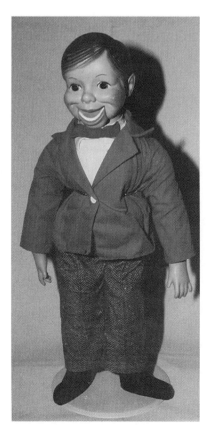

23" "Willie Talk" made of cloth with vinyl gauntlet hands and plastic head. Pull string operated mouth. Original, 1978. Marked "Horsman, Inc./25." $50.00.

23" "Emmet Kelly" pull string talker. Cloth and plastic. Original. Marked "Horsman Doll/1978/6-3." $60.00.

12" "Randy" made of plastic and vinyl with sleep eyes and rooted hair. Original. Designed by Irene Szor for Horsman Doll Co. Ca. 1980. $25.00.

8" "Lavender Ballerina" with silver crown. Sleep eyes with painted lashes below eyes only. Marked "Intre-D. 1982." Tagged "Horsman Doll." $20.00.

11½" "Nadia Ballerina" made of plastic and vinyl with sleep eyes, rooted hair, and cute face. Made by Horsman in 1987. $20.00.

17" "Ronald Reagan" made of plastic and vinyl with open/closed mouth and molded hair. Marked "1987/RRA18." Tagged "Horsman." $65.00.

10½" "HeBee" made of plastic and vinyl that looks exactly like composition. Has molded-on white undies. Painted features. Limited edition, marked "1987 Horsman." $50.00.

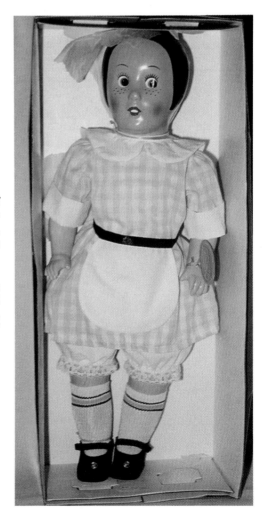

Left: 18" "Pert 'n Pretty" made of plastic and vinyl. Has knob on lower back that works grow hair feature. Marked "H-6-17/Horsman/1988/Made in China." $48.00.

Right: 17" "Ella Cinder." Composition look and feel but made of vinyl and plastic. Painted features and hair. Made in 1988. Tagged "Horsman." $90.00.

7½" "Summer" is made of plastic and vinyl with sleep eyes. Original. Marked "Horsman 1988. Made in Hong Kong" on body. $35.00.

7½" "Winter" is made of plastic and vinyl with brown sleep eyes. Original. Marked "Horsman 1988. Made in Hong Kong" on body. $35.00.

14" "Mary Hoyer" doll made of all hard plastic and never played with. (Full length photo in *Patricia Smith's Doll Values*, Volume 7, page 241.) The original wedding gown exceeds excellent. Has about four foot train that attaches to dress at waist sides. This particular doll - $1,200.00. Other Hoyer dolls, clean and original: hard plastic - $485.00; composition - $500.00.

Left to right: "Howdy Doody" bean bag with vinyl head and hands. Partially hidden by "Clarabelle the Clown." Made by Eegee in 1973. $45.00. 20" "Howdy Doody" with cloth body and vinyl head, feet, and hands. Made by Eegee in 1973. $95.00 Back center: 12" "Howdy Doody" cloth/vinyl doll with pull string for mouth. Made by Eegee in 1973. $45.00. 20" "Howdy Doody" made of all cloth with hard plastic features and pull string mouth. Made by Ideal, 1950. $185.00. 26" "Howdy Doody" with cloth body, plastic head and hands, and pull string mouth. Made by Eegee, 1973. $200.00. Front: 16" "Howdy Doody" with vinyl head, cloth body, and felt gloves/boots. Maker unknown. $90.00. 28" "Howdy Doody" with composition head and hands and sleep eyes. Made by Effanbee. $300.00.

Hummel

Hummel dolls were made by William Goebel in Germany from 1948 into the 1950s. The first dolls were made of all rubber. Later, vinyl dolls were made from the same molds. All of these dolls will have deeply molded hair and painted features and look very much like the Hummel porcelain figures. Their heads are marked, and they wear tagged clothes. The early dolls will have a triangle wrist tag, and the later ones have a round tag. Generally, they are 12 – 16" sizes.

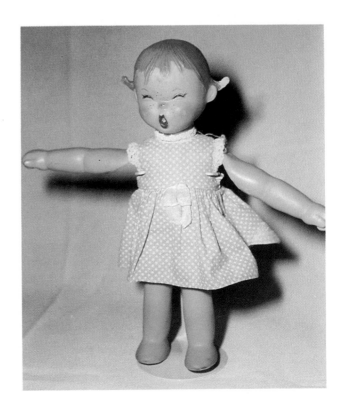

Right: 9½" doll made of all vinyl with freckles and painted half closed eyes. Wide open/closed mouth with molded tongue. Has very unusual joints. Upper arms are flat underneath. Ca. 1970s. Marked "Bee/"V"-Goebel/Charlotte Bye (designer) 2916" on head. Body marked "W. Goebel/3906/Goebel mark/W. Germany/GESCH./D.R.G.M. 1914035." $60.00.

12" marked Hummel girl and boy dolls made of rubber and in excellent condition. Quality of the clothes on these early dolls is far better than the later ones. Skin tones will be darker with more orange tones than the vinyl dolls. Each - $185.00.

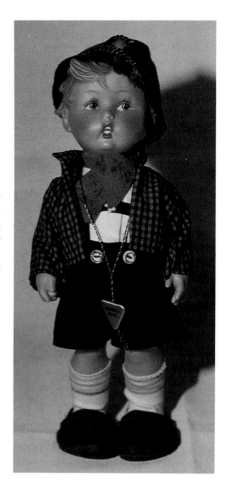

11" girl and 12" boy made of all vinyl with round tags. Ca. 1980s. Marked "Hummel" with bee mark and large "V/Goebel." Each - $165.00.

Ideal Doll Company

There are two dolls that come to mind for any collector when Ideal dolls are mentioned – "Shirley Temple" and "Toni." The success of the Shirley Temple dolls was a shining highlight in the company's 86-year doll-making history.

Ideal has made the majority of collectible dolls over all the material years (composition, hard plastic, vinyl) with no competition. You say, "What about Madame Alexander?" Madame Alexander dolls were *very expensive*, and from the 1930s to the 1970s, the dolls were sold through fine department stores and exclusive children's stores. During that period the only other stores carrying dolls were local or chain department stores and catalog firms such as Sears-Roebuck and Montgomery Ward. Therefore, affordable dolls, such as those produced by Ideal, were available to the average child.

Since Madame Alexander dolls sold in a different market, Ideal's main competition was the American Character and Arranbee doll companies. These two companies survived for many years, but finally yielded to Ideal's everlasting appeal.

The composition of Ideal dolls compares with that of the finest dolls. Starting with Shirley Temple, the list of excellent dolls includes Deanna Durbin, Judy Garland, Pinocchio, Snoosie, and many more. Dolls made in the hard plastic era are some of the most collectible and the hardest to find! During the plastic/vinyl period, Ideal dolls have some of the prettiest hands ever designed by any company. Ideal Dolls made great quality dolls up to the 1980s.

Collecting Ideal dolls can be a lot of fun. Any group, such as the "Patty Playpal" group, the Crissy group, Tammy and her family, Toni/Harriet Hubbart Ayers dolls, the Mary Hartline group, or the many different Thumblina dolls, would be fun to search and collect. The excellence of Ideal dolls makes their collectibility well deserved.

22" "Flossie Flirt" made of cloth and composition with sleep, flirty eyes. Red mohair wig. Early 1930s. Marked with "Ideal" in diamond on head. Mint - $300.00 up.

Left: 22" "Mary Lou" made of all composition, sleep eyes, and open mouth. All original. Mid-1930s. Marked with "Ideal" in diamond/USA. $385.00 up. Right: 19" "Mary Ann" has Patsy-style body. Hair combed out, replaced clothes. Name marked on her head along with "Effanbee." $285.00 up.

19" "Plassie" with hard plastic head, sleep eyes, and molded hair. Cloth body with composition limbs. Original. Marked "Ideal Doll/Made in U.S.A./Pa No. 2252077," on head "1949." Mint - $175.00; soiled - $65.00.

14" "Plassie" is made of all hard plastic with deeply molded hair. Sleep eyes with lashes. From 1952. Marked "Ideal Doll/Made in U.S.A." on head and "Ideal Doll/14" on body. $60.00.

18" "Miss Revlon" is vinyl with blue sleep eyes, jointed waist, and high heel feet. Both original in striped dresses. marked "Ideal Doll."1958. Mint - $175.00.

20–21" P-93 "Toni" with blonde nylon hair and sleep eyes. Perfect copy of an original outfit. $485.00 up.

9" "Dodi" made of all vinyl with bendable arms and legs. Painted features with smile mouth and painted teeth. Shown in original box. Goes with the Tammy and Pepper family, 1964. In box - $55.00. Doll only, mint - $40.00.

15" "Fashion Liz" made of plastic and vinyl with eyes painted to side. Dressed in bikini bathing suit. (Same doll as Tammy's mom.) From 1965. $55.00 up.

17" "Posie" is foam-filled doll with vinyl half arms and head. Has sleep eyes and in original dress. Marked "1967 Ideal Toy Corp./F-18-E-H-E4." $38.00.

25" "Miss Ideal" with plastic body and legs, sleep eyes/lashes, and closed smiling mouth. Vinyl arms and head. Extra joints at wrists, waist, and ankles. Marked "Ideal Toy Corp/SP-25-S"; on head "1961." Mint - $425.00.

12" "Captain Action" made of plastic and vinyl with multi-jointed body. Marked "1966/ Ideal Toy Corp." In oval, "H-93." On back, "1966/Ideal Toy Corp/8." $80.00 up.

9" "Action Boy" made of plastic and vinyl with multi-jointed body. Excellent facial detail and hair modeling. Original, from "Captain Action" set. Marked "1966/Ideal Toy Corp" on head. Body marked "1987/Ideal Toy Corp." $70.00 up.

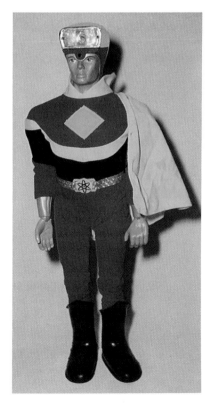

16" "Electro-Man" has "...electronic brain that works like a calculator." Battery operated with lights and sounds. His enemy is an ape-like creature called "Zogg." Marked "Ideal 1977." $95.00 up.

18" "Tara" was sold and marketed in leftover "Electro-Man" uniforms. Marked "1977/Ideal/M.H.C. 19-H-230/Hong Kong." $55.00.

12" "Knight of Darkness" is a multi-jointed action figure. Original, from the Zeroid Star Team. Marked "1977 Ideal HHP-H-285" and body marked "Hong Kong." $45.00 up.

16" "Tippy Tumbles." (Boy is "Tommy Tumbles.") Plastic and vinyl with battery in plastic case attached. Marked "1976/Ideal Toy Corp./7-IGG-H-276." $38.00.

14" "Kit" made of cloth with vinyl gauntlet hands, vinyl head, and plastic boots. Has painted features. 17" "Kabott" is her battery-operated horse. 1977. Both - $55.00; Doll only - $3.00.

13" "Whoopsie." Press tummy and her braids fly up. Marked "Ideal Toy Corp./Hong Kong/1978/N-2-377." $35.00.

12" "Pretty Curls" made of all vinyl with painted features. Marked "Ideal/1980/H-341." Body marked "Ideal Toy Corp./ 1980/B-95." $35.00.

16" "Betsy ®" made of all white vinyl with bright pink lips and sleep eyes. From 1982. Marked "Ideal/1982/C.B.S. Inc. 387." $18.00.

13" "Betsy Wetsy ®." This was during their "white" period after the company was sold to Columbia Broadcasting Company. Almost all doll makers during the early 1980s thought the "white," rather than the skin-toned dolls, were the best to make. From 1984. Marked "Ideal CBS Inc." $18.00.

12" "Charlotte" is one of the "Victorian Ladies." These ladies also came in 8" size. Made of white vinyl. Marked "1982/Ideal Toy Corp./H 374" on head. Body marked "Ideal" in oval, 1983/C.B.S. Toys. $20.00.

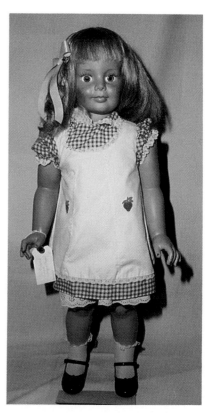

36" "Patty Playpal" made of plastic and vinyl with inset eyes and lashes. Original. Reintroduced 1986. Marked "Ideal G-35/H-346" on head. $85.00.

16" "Rub-A-Dub Dolly" made of all vinyl with inset eyes/lashes. Original in box. One of the "Nursery Group" from 1989. $28.00.

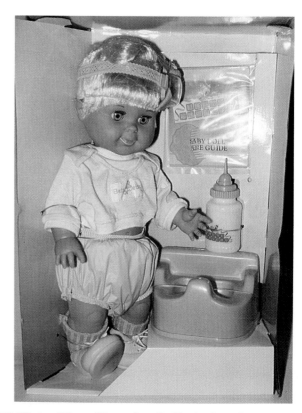

16" "Betsy Wetsy ®" made of all vinyl with inset eyes/lashes. Came with potty chair. Original in box. From 1989. $29.00.

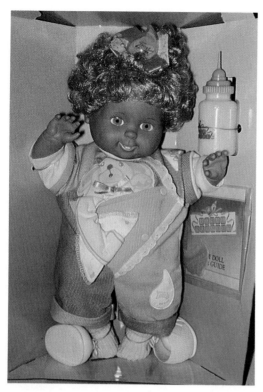

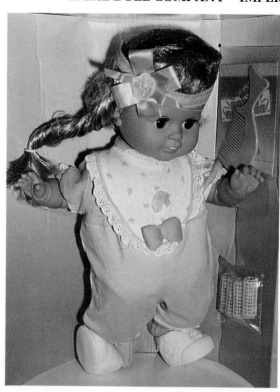

16" "Tiny Tears" of the "Nursery Group," Cloth and vinyl with inset eyes. Original in box. From 1989. $28.00.

Tiny 16" "Crissy Baby®" made of cloth and vinyl with frosted orange and white rooted hair. Open/closed mouth with teeth. Inset eyes/lashes. Original in box. From 1989. $32.00.

7" "Alien" from the movie *Close Encounters of the Third Kind.* All vinyl and bendable. Made by Imperial Toy Corp. in 1977. $16.00.

7" Desert Storm dolls made for The Salvation Army's "Operation We Care." Limited editions by In Time Productions. Made in China, 1991. Left: General Norman Schwarzkopf - $28.00; Center: General Colin Powell - $28.00. Right: President George Bush - $32.00.

6" all plastic doll with sleep eyes. Molded-on green dress, shoes, and socks. Legs swing from hips and arms rotate. Made by Irwin Plastics, ca. 1960. $20.00.

24" "Sweet Susan" made of cloth and vinyl with sleep eyes/lashes. One of "Second Generation Babies." Four dolls in set. Limited production, dolls are numbered. Marked "Loving Legacy Dolls/by JPI 1989/NY, NY 10003, U.S.A." $68.00.

11" "Kewpie" made of all vinyl. Original. Made by Jesco in late 1980s. $36.00.

8" "Kewpie" made of all vinyl with painted features. Original. Made by Jesco. $28.00.

11" "Scootles" with modeled hair and sweet smile. Original. Made by Jesco. Head marked "Cameo/Hong Kong." $30.00.

9½" "Katie" with smiling closed mouth and sleep eyes. Had a large selection of packaged extra outfits available. Marked "Jesco 1984." $25.00.

5½" "Nancy Ann Storybook." Reintroduced. All rigid plastic that is jointed at hips, shoulders, and neck. Painted features. Marked "Nancy Ann Dolls/Jesco Inc./1985/China." $18.00.

18" "Twistee Posie" named "Dixie Pixie." Cloth covered foam with vinyl head and gauntlet hands. Large sleep eyes, open/closed mouth with painted upper teeth. Rooted hair. Marked "Jolly Toys Inc. 1964." $40.00.

11" doll made of all composition with oversized hair bow style hat. Original. Eyes were painted straight ahead as well to the side. Made by Junel in 1946. $65.00.

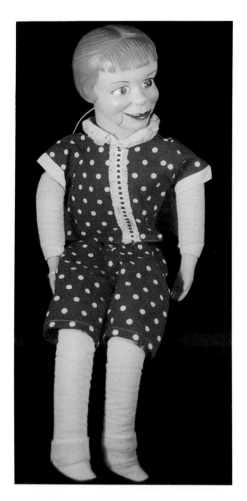

28" girl puppet is all cloth with vinyl head and molded hair. Painted features, string operated mouth. Marked "1968/Juro Novelty/Co. Inc." $85.00.

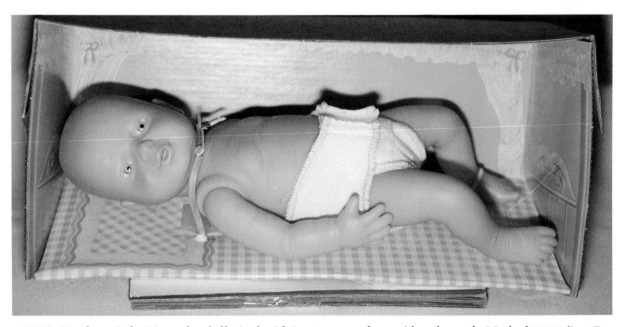

10" "My Newborn Baby" is made of all vinyl with inset eyes and open/closed mouth. Marked "1986/Just For You (H.K.)" on head and "1986 Made Just For Kids" on box. $48.00.

Left: 20" "Catherine" with long thin limbs and high heel feet. Plastic body and legs. Vinyl head with blonde hair and sleep eyes/lashes. Original, made by Kaysam in 1986. $95.00 up.

Right: 14" plastic and vinyl doll with sleep eyes. Open/closed mouth, blonde hair. Marked "C.P.G. Products Corp. 1070/ Made in Hong Kong" on head and "Kenner Div.-2-1979" on body. $32.00.

13" "Baby Teefoam" made of all vinyl. Painted features, open/closed mouth. Cryer, press arms or legs and she won't cry. Marked "G.M.F.G.I. 1978." Made by Kenner. $42.00.

17" "Nancy Nonsense" made of plastic and vinyl with smile and freckles. Pull string talker. Large painted eyes. Marked "Kenner Products 1974" on head; "1974/General Mills Fun Groups Inc./Div. of Kenner Prod. Co." $40.00.

4" mermaid made of plastic and vinyl. Lower body inside sponge. Shown with baby mermaid. Marked "C.P.G. Kenner 1979 Hong Kong." Complete set - $22.00.

6" "Tickles and Gigglet" made of all vinyl. Marked "1986 Hallmark Cards, Inc. Kenner. Made in China." Body marked "1986 Hallmark Cards, Inc." Baby marked "8G.H.C.I." Complete set - $25.00.

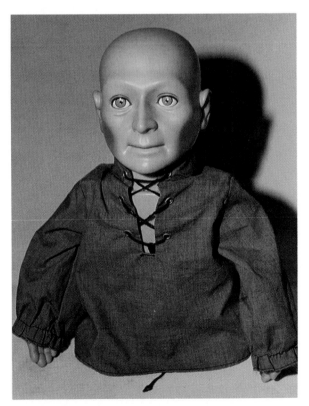

12" "Dr. Hugo" hand puppet. Plastic and vinyl with cloth upper arms. Came with disguise kit and called "Man of a Thousand Faces." Marked "M.F.G.I./1975" on head. Front marked "1975 General Mills Fun Group by its division Kenner Products/Made in Hong Kong." $45.00.

13" "Six Million Dollar Man" in astronaunt uniform. Multi-jointed body and "bionic" eye. Marked "Universal City Studios, Inc/1973/All Rights Reserved. General Mills Fun Group, Inc. by Div. Kenner Products. $60.00.

Left: 12" "Erica" with plastic and vinyl multi-jointed body and red hair. Marked "C.P.F.G.I. Products Corp. 1978/Kenner/Hong Kong." $35.00. Center: 12" "Darcie" with multi-jointed body and blonde hair. Marked "C.P.G. Products Corp. 1978/Kenner Cincinnati. Made in Hong Kong." $35.00. Right: 12" "Darcie Cover Girl" with plastic and vinyl body jointed at wrists, knees, and waist. Blonde hair. Marked "Kenner 1978/G.M.F.G.I./1978/Made in Hong Kong. $35.00.

3" "Mini-Kins" dolls resemble plastic paper dolls with painted features, shoes, and undies. Plastic clothes and articles are molded plastic that fit over the front of the doll. Marked "K.T.C. 1979 Made in Hong Kong Pat #4227840/0408102" or can be "K.T.C. 1981-H.I." with patent number or other Pat. Pending and "Made in Hong Kong." Some may also me marked with the number "H-17." Doll only - $7.00; Doll with one outfit - $12.00; Complete set - $65.00.

3" "Mini-kins" dolls styled like plastic paper dolls. Note various outfits and hairstyles. Made by K.T.C. in 1979. Marks information and prices on previous page.

3" "Mini-Kins" with clothes that fit over the doll with opening for face. (Doll information and pricing on page 154.)

3" "Mini-Kins" dolls with fitted-on clothes and accessories. Above: Both dolls are riding bicycles. Below: Doll on left sits at table with birthday cake. On right, doll is sitting cross-legged in chair. (See page 154 for information and pricing.)

5½" "Strawberry Shortcake" of 1980. Came with cat "Custard." $12.00.

"Baby Strawberry Shortcake" of 1981. $14.00.

Left: This "Raspberry Tart" doll came with bear-like animal called "Rhubarb." 1980. Set - $10.00. Center: "Blueberry Muffin." 1980. Wears plastic hat. $10.00. Right: 5½" "Orange Blossom" and "Marmalade" from 1981. Set - $10.00.

5½" "Cherry Cobbler" and "Gooseberry." 1980 – 1984. Set - $12.00.

"Baby Butter Cookie" and "Jelly Bear." Set - $12.00.

"Baby Apricot" and "Hopsolot." Original, 1980 – 1984. Set - $12.00.

5½" "Angel Cake" and "Soufflé." Original, 1980 – 1984. Set - $12.00.

"Huckleberry Pie" and "Pupcake." Set - $12.00.

"Lemon Meringue" and "Frappé." Original. Set - $12.00.

5½" "Strawberry Shortcake" with her cat, "Custard." "Berry Cycle" came packaged separately. 1984. Doll/cat set - $12.00; Cycle - $10.00.

"Dancing Strawberry Shortcake" from 1983. Set - $15.00.

"Baby Lemon" and "Baby Lime Chiffon" abroad "Flutter Bit Butterfly" from 1982. Dolls, each - $12.00; Butterfly - $15.00.

Boy doll on left is "Almond Tea" with purple hair. Girl on right is "Mint Tulip" with yellow hair. Shown with animals "Marsh Mallard" and "Marza Panda." (Bear also came in white with lavender tail and back legs.) Donkey "Burrito" is part of the "Cafe Olé" set. The doll in that set wore a poncho and had green/white strip socks. 1983. Each set - $12.00.

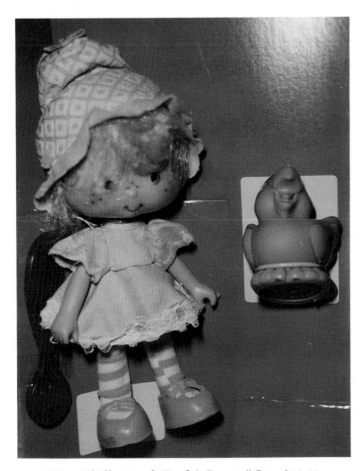

"Lime Chiffon" and "Parfait Parrot." Set - $12.00.

"Apple Dumpling." Came with "Tea Time Turtle." Set - $12.00.

5½" "Strawberry Shortcake" friends with sleep eyes. Made in 1984 only. Left: "Orange Blossom" and sleeping "Marmalade." Has sleeping bag. Right: "Blueberry Tart" in original sleeping bag. Both dolls - $35.00.

5½" "Lemon Meringue" with frog "Frappe." Has sleep eyes and shown in original package. Made in 1984 only. $35.00 up.

Left: 8½" "Purple Pieman" and "Berry Bird." Right: 8½" "Dregs" with purple hair and blue chiffon scarf. Strawberry Shortcake's foes were introduced in 1982. Each - $15.00.

18" "Precious Hugs" with inset eyes, soft plush body. From Hugga Baby group. Made for Hallmark Cards in 1985 by Kenner Products. $42.00.

16" "Beetlejuice" is a cloth and vinyl doll with pull string talker. From movie of same name. Marked "Kenner 1989. The Gefkin Co. Kenner, Div. of Tonka Corp." $30.00.

16" "Ernest" is a pull string talker made of cloth and vinyl. T-shirt is imprinted with the doll's name. Removable clothes and hat. Marked "Kenner Div. of Tonka Corp. 1989." $42.00.

4½" "Glamour Gals" with molded-on clothes and had extra outfits available. All will be marked "1981" or "1982 C.P.G. Made by Kenner." Each - $12.00.

4½" "Glamour Gals" made of plastic and vinyl. Some have molded slacks or complete outfits while others have molded-on undies or swimsuits. They had extensive extra packaged wardrobes available for them. All will be marked "1981" or "1982 C.P.G. Made by Kenner." Each - $12.00.

5" plastic and vinyl doll with painted features. Original. Marked "Kid Co./1981" on body. $8.00.

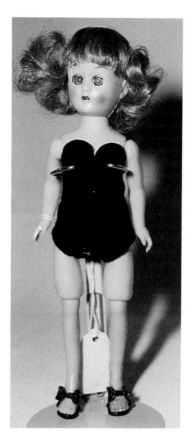

8" "Kim" made of all hard plastic with jointed knees, sleep eyes, and glued-on wig. Marked "Kim Dolls, N.Y. 1954." $15.00.

16" "Popeye" made of cloth and vinyl. Original, marked "King Features Inc./Popeye" on head. 1987. $65.00.

Left: 9" and 8" dolls made of all felt with painted features. Original. Made by Klumpe. Each - $85.00. Rightt: 8" Nurse and Doctor. Both are original. (There is also a nurse and a doctor that hold a baby.) Made by Klumpe of Spain. Each - $95.00.

Two all felt dolls with posable limbs and painted features. Both original. Made by Klumpe of Spain. Each - $95.00.

14" "Dagwood" and 9" "Alexander." Both are all composition with molded hair and painted features. Removable clothes except shoes and socks on "Alexander." Both all original dolls are marked "Knickerbocker" on their heads. "Dagwood" - $650.00 up; "Alexander" - $375.00 up.

11" "Holly Hobbie" doll made of all vinyl with little facial detail and painted eyes. Original in green clothes and straw hat. Marked "K.T.C. 1975/Made in Taiwan" on head and back. Made by Knickerbocker Toy Co. $12.00.

10" and 6" "Annie" dolls. Both are original. Marked "1982 Tribune Company" on body and "Knickerbocker Toy Co. Inc." on head. Small doll can be marked "1982 CPI Inc./1982 Knickerbocker Toy Co., Inc. H-15." 10" - $15.00; 6" - $7.00.

11½" "Michael Jackson" doll has jointed waist and bendable knees. Separate outfits were available. Marked "1984 MJJ Productions/L.J.N. Toys Ltd." $20.00.

11½" action figure from the television series "V." Knob on back makes tongue come out. Extra joints at waist, elbows, and knees. Marked "1984/Warner Bros./L.J.N. Toys, Ltd." $60.00.

11½" "Flo Jo" Fashion Doll (Florence Griffith Joyner) has bendable knees. Made by L.J.N. Toys, Ltd. Marked "1989" on head. $28.00.

Figures from the movie *Gremlins*. Left photo shows different sizes of "Gizmo." In the center foreground is "Stripe." When "Stripe" ate after midnight, he turned into the bad gremlin shown in right photo. Figures marked "Warner Bros. 1984/L.J.N Toys Ltds. Each - $22.00 up.

Left: 9" "Harlem Globetrotter" made of all vinyl and completely bendable. Made by Lakeside in 1987. $10.00.

Right: 6" "Bozo The Clown" bendy made of all vinyl and fully posable. Marked "Bozo Clown/Larry Harmon/Pictures Corp./Capitol Records, Inc./Mfg for Lakeside Ind./Made in Hong Kong." 1972. $13.00.

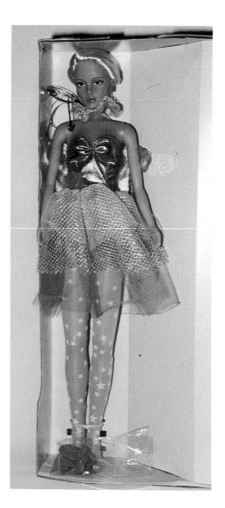

Left: 17" "Glitter" made of plastic and vinyl with painted features. Marked "Lanard 1987." $80.00.

Right: 17" "Nina" made of plastic and vinyl with painted features. One of the "Jet Setters." Four dolls in set. Marked "Lanard 1987." $80.00.

14" baby is plastic and vinyl with rooted hair and painted features. Marked "1973 Lesney/Made in Hong Kong." $28.00.

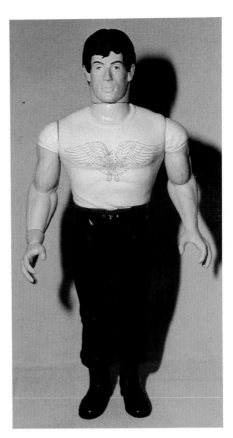

Sylvester Stallone as "Lincoln Hawks." Arms activated by knob on back. Also available with jointed elbows. From the movie *Over The Top.* Marked "1986 Cannon Films Inc./All Rights Reserved/Lewco, New York 10010/Made in China." $15.00.

Left: 17" "Lorrie Toddler" is made of plastic and vinyl with sleep eyes/lashes and has pink lip color. Original. Made in 1988. Marked "Lorrie Doll." $18.00.

Right: 19" "Sweet Candy" made of plastic and vinyl with sleep eyes and open mouth. Head is modeled slightly downward. Marked "Lorrie Doll 1964." $28.00.

9", 12", and 16" "Loving Sister" from the "Dreamland Series." Vinyl and plastic dolls with sleep eyes and blonde curly hair. The 16" size has a cloth body with vinyl head and limbs. Marked "1988 Lucky Ind. Co., Ltd. N.Y." Set - $32.00.

11" "Betty Boop" made of all vinyl with deeply modeled hair and painted features. Original. Marked "Marty Toy 1986." $29.00.

Left: 11½" "Janie West" and "Captain Tom Maddox." Both have blue molded-on clothes and separate vinyl accesories. Jointed at elbows and knees. (Dark hair girl is "Josie West.") Marked "Marx MCMLXVII (1967)." Each - $18.00. Right: 11½" "Geronimo" without face mask and "Johnny West." Cowboy has tan molded-on clothes and brown extra clothes made of vinyl. Marked "Marx Toys 1967." Each - $20.00.

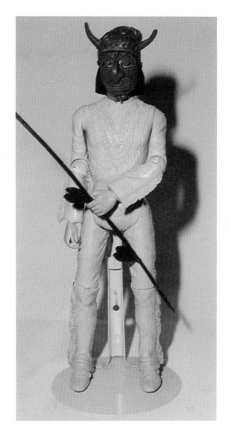

11½" "Geronimo" came with face mask and lance. Marked "Marx Toys. 1967." $25.00.

9" "Betty" and "Archie" made of all vinyl with painted features. "Archie" has modeled hair and "Betty" has long blonde rooted hair. Both marked "Made in Hong Kong/Marx/1975." Each - $12.00.

Right: 9" "Reggie" and "Veronica" from the "Archie" group. Both marked "Made in Hong Kong/Marx/1975." Each - $12.00.

2" "Butterfly Princess" clip-on jewelry. Excellent quality for so tiny a doll. Vinyl with molded bodice. Six dolls in set. This one is "Lilac" with lavender clothes. Others are "Magnolia," "Periwinkle," "Daffodil," "Azalea," and "Rosebud." Marked "Matchbox. 1988." Each - $10.00.

Left: 18" "Pee-Wee Herman" made of cloth and vinyl and is a pull string talker. Marked "Matchbox. 1987." $85.00. Right: 24" "Pee-Wee Herman" made of cloth with plastic lower legs and molded-on shoes. Plastic lower arms, vinyl head, painted features and hair. Pull string in back operates mouth. Marked "Matchbox. 1989." $85.00.

19" "Billy Baloney" made of cloth and plastic. Pull string operates mouth and eyes. From the "Pee-Wee Herman Show." Marked "Matchbox/Lic. Harmon Toys, Inc. 1988." $60.00.

Mattel, Inc.

When "Mattel" is mentioned, the majority of the people think of "Barbie." True, she has been their foundation and cornerstone for almost 45 years (1959 – 1994), but Mattel also made many delightful, highly collectible dolls during the same period. These dolls range from their line of baby dolls to the Kiddles.

Barbie is a highly stylized area of collecting, and serious collectors have let Barbie have 100% of their attention. They have spent many years researching her background and collection. There are many books on the market that are dedicated only to Barbie and her friends. In fact, there are three books that can be ordered from Collector Books concerning Barbie. They are authored by Susan Manos and Sarah Sink Eames.

Since this book covers general information for collectors, an overview has been given for Mattel dolls, including Barbie.

"Barbie Wedding Party Gift Set" included four dolls – "Barbie," "Ken," "Skipper," and "Midge." Very rare. $1,300.00 up.

Mix and Match Set of 1962 included a boxed "Barbie" and extensive wardrobe. Any of the boxed gift sets are very rare. $1,000.00 up.

Left: "Angel Face Barbie." White lace bodice and sleeves with pink long skirt. From 1966. $30.00 up. Center: "Kissing Barbie" in extra boxed outfit. Came with lipstick. Kisses were given by placing her lips on Ken's cheek and pressing button on back. Kiss imprint was left. From 1979. $50.00 up. Right: "Gift Giving Barbie" in pink and silver dress. From 1985. $40.00.

Left: "Pool Side Barbie" in yellow with red/blue sash and "Uptown Barbie" in pink gown with silver belt. Both are from 1966. Each - $40.00. Right: "Party Cruise Barbie" with multi-colored bodice and white skirt. "Funtime Barbie" in two-piece short suit. Pink earrings and bracelet. Both from 1986. Each - $35.00.

Left: "Perfume Pretty Barbie." Dressed in all pink. Came with Barbie perfume. From 1987. $30.00. Right: "Perfume Giving Ken" Taupe slacks, silver/white tuxedo jacket with light mauve cummerbund and tie. From 1986. $25.00.

"Perfume Pretty Whitney" has reddish-brown hair and very pale blue dress. Made in China in 1987. $20.00.

"Barbie and The Sensations." Bright pink and white outfit. Came with cassette. From 1987. $30.00.

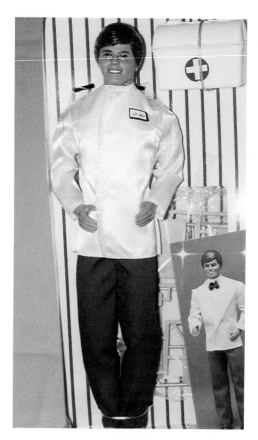

Left: "Doctor Barbie." Pink dress changes into evening gown. White lab coat. From 1986. $20.00.
Right: "Doctor Ken." Navy slacks. Lab coat reverses into tuxedo coat. From 1987. $20.00.

Left: "Jewel Secret Barbie." White bodice and pink/silver striped skirt. Right: "Jewel Secret Ken." Silver suit with vivid blue cummerbund and bowtie. Both dolls rom 1986. Each - $25.00.

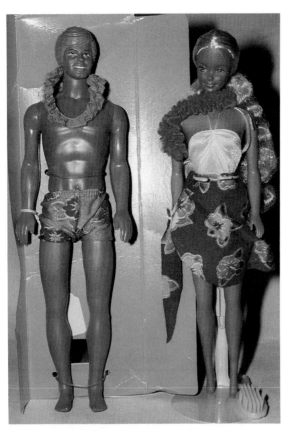

Left: "Island Fun Ken and Barbie." This "Barbie" has the typical head. From 1987. Right: "Island Fun Skipper and Kira." "Skipper" has oversized blue eyes and Kira has Polynesian eyes. From 1987. Each - $15.00.

Left: "California Dream Barbie" dressed in yellow, blue, and pink print outfit. From 1987. $15.00.

Right: "California Dream Ken" dressed in yellow striped top and red polka dot trunks. From 1987. $15.00.

181

"Super Hair Barbie" dressed in white two-piece western outfit. From 1986. $30.00.

"Sun Lovin' Malibu Barbie" in blue two-piece bathing suit. Has tan lines. From 1979. "Fun To Dress Barbie" in pale pink bra and panties. From 1987. Each - $12.00.

Left to right: "Hostess Barbie" in lavender dress with white trim. From 1986; "Fashion Play Barbie" in white dress with multi-colored design. Dress makes two outfits. From 1987; "Fashion Play Barbie" in bright pink dress. From 1987; "Fashion Play Barbie" in blue dress. From 1988. Each - $15.00.

Left: "Style Magic Barbie." Pink bodice and dotted skirt and collar. From 1988. $15.00.

Right: "Solo in the Spotlight" porcelain Barbie from 1989. $350.00 up.

Left: "Super Star Ken" dressed in silver and white tuxedo with pink cummerbund. Has trophy. From 1988. $25.00. Right: "50th Anniversary Ice Capades Ken" dressed in aqua, white, and pink skater's costume. Made in Malaysia. From 1989. $30.00.

11½" "Super Star Barbie." Pink skirt and white bodice covered with silver stars. From 1988. $35.00.

Left: "Happy Holidays Barbie" Special Edition – 1988. First in series. Dressed all in red. $200.00 up. Right: "Happy Holidays Barbie" Special Edition – 1989. Second in series. All white dress with "fur" trim. $125.00.

Left: "Happy Holidays Barbie" Special Edition – 1990. Third in series. Dressed all in pink. Made in China. $85.00 up. Right: "Wedding Fantasy Barbie." Made in China. From 1989. $20.00.

Left: "Mexican Barbie" has brown hair and eyes. Dressed in red and white outfit with white lace mantilla. From 1988. $75.00.

Right: "Nigerian Barbie" has brown eyes and black hair. Tan, brown, and blue animal print dress. From 1989. $55.00.

Left: 11½" "DeeDee" and "Diva" from "Barbie and The Rockers." Spandex style outfits. Made in Taiwan, 1986. $150.00 up. Right: "Western Fun Mia." Blue/white outfit. Long brown braid. From 1989. $20.00.

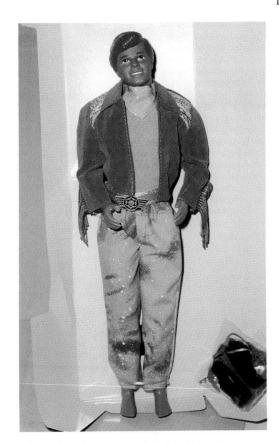

"Western Fun Barbie and Ken." Blue and pink outfits. From 1989. Each - $20.00.

"Flight Time Barbie and Ken." "Barbie" wears pink pilot uniform. Separate accessories converts uniform into outift for off-duty hours. "Ken" wears blue pilot uniform. Added accessories for evening wear. From 1989. Each - $25.00.

Right: "Navy Barbie." White uniform with navy trim. First new military issue from 1989. $35.00. Left: "Air Force Barbie." Olive green jumpsuit with brown "leather" flight jacket. Second military issue from 1990. $25.00. Below: "Army Barbie." Dressed in formal evening uniform. Set comes with daywear. Third military issue from 1990. $25.00.

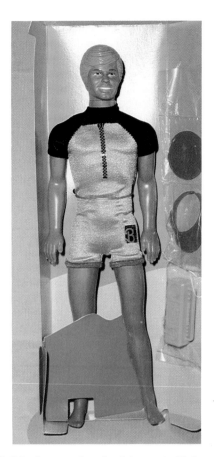

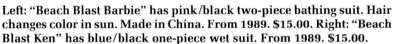

Left: "Beach Blast Barbie" has pink/black two-piece bathing suit. Hair changes color in sun. Made in China. From 1989. $15.00. Right: "Beach Blast Ken" has blue/black one-piece wet suit. From 1989. $15.00.

"Feeling Fun Barbie." Blue with pink lace overshirt. From 1988. $15.00.

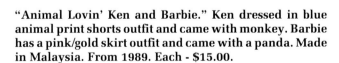

"Animal Lovin' Ken and Barbie." Ken dressed in blue animal print shorts outfit and came with monkey. Barbie has a pink/gold skirt outfit and came with a panda. Made in Malaysia. From 1989. Each - $15.00.

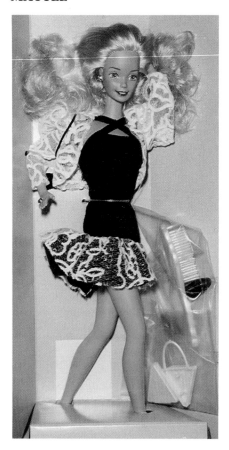

Left: "Party Pretty Barbie." Dressed in short black and white evening outfit with matching lace jacket. From 1990. $20.00.

Right: "American Beauty Queen Barbie." Blue/silver formal converts into tutu for talent show competition and swimsuit. Made in China. From 1990. $20.00.

"Homecoming Queen Skipper." Large round painted eyes. All white gown. From 1988. $35.00.

"Babysitter Skipper." Skipper dressed in pink/white polka dot outfit. Baby made in Malaysia. From 1991. $15.00.

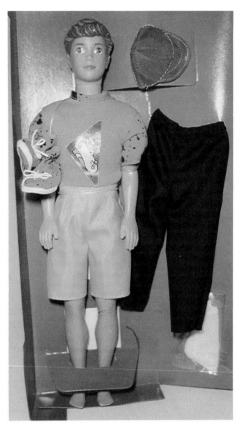

"Kevin" is the teen boyfriend of "Skipper." Blue/yellow outfit with extra black slacks and hot pink cap. $15.00.

"Stacey" and "Todd" serve as flowergirl and ringbearer for "Wedding Party" set. Todd has flocked hair. Both have freckles. $22.00.

3" and 1" "Mr. & Mrs. Little and Baby." All vinyl. Larger dolls marked "Mattel/ 1980/Hawthrone." Baby marked "Made in Taiwan." Complete set - $18.00.

Left: 11½" "Ann Margaret" with painted features with open/closed smiling mouth. Original. Marked "Mattel, Inc./1966/Korea." $30.00.

Right: Black "Heart Family." Mother/daughter outfits are pale pink. Father and son are dressed in blue/white clothes. Accessories included. From 1984. Complete set - $45.00.

Heart Family's "Schooltime Fun" set. Left: 11½" teacher/mother and 4" boy. Right: 12" coach/father and 4" girl. Made by Mattel in China, 1988. Each set - $28.00.

16" "Baby Pat-A-Cake." Cloth legs, vinyl arms and head, soft vinyl bottom. Molded-on clothes, plastic potty chair. Doll modeled in sitting position. Pull string to clap hands if she wets. Open mouth nurser. Marked "Mattel/1981/ Made in Mexico." Doll/potty - $30.00; Doll only - $18.00.

18" "Rainbow Brite" made of vinyl and cloth. Stitched fingers. Head marked "1983 Hallmark Cards, Inc. Taiwan." $30.00. Shown with 11" plush "Twinkle Sprite" tagged "Mattel 1983." $10.00.

Left: 18" "Patty O'Green," friend of "Rainbow Brite." Has freckles. Marked "1983 Hallmark Cards, Inc. Taiwan." $35.00. Shown with red/green "Lucky Sprite" tagged "Mattel 1983." $25.00.

Right: 18" lavender doll is friend of "Rainbow Brite." Yarn hair and molded-on glass. Marked the same as other dolls in set. $35.00.

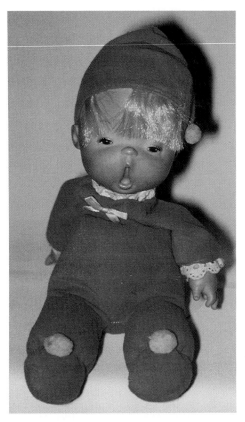

10" "Yawning Beans" has tuffs of hair and painted sleepy eyes. Original. Marked "1970/Mattel, Inc." $12.00.

10" "Baby Love Notes" plays different tunes by pressing hands, feet, and body. Vinyl head. Marked "Mattel, Inc./ 1974." $15.00.

Left: 14" "Hush Lil' Baby" made of all vinyl with painted features. Marked "Mattel Inc. 1976/U.S.A." $28.00.

Right: 14" "Baby Cries For You" waves and cries when pull string is activated. Also came in black version. Marked "1979/Mattel, Inc." $25.00.

Left: 13" "Dimples" made of plastic and vinyl with very chubby short legs. Marked "1980/ Mattel, Inc./Mexico" on head and "Mattel, Inc./ 1988/Mexico" on body. $18.00.

Right: 18" plastic and vinyl doll with unique neck joint. Pull string makes arms move and head extend. Marked "Mattel, Inc. 1978." $22.00.

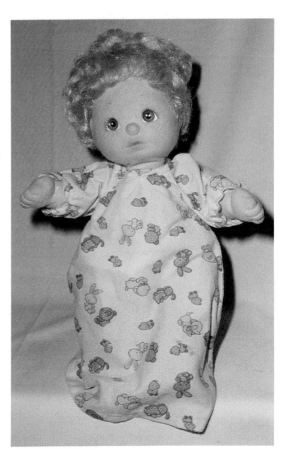

Left: 15" "Crawling Baby" made of plastic and vinyl and is key operated. Original. Marked "Mattel/ 1984." $18.00.

Right: 15" "My Child" has flannel body and head with stitched fingers. Had many different outfits. Tag marked "Mattel, Inc./1985/ Made in China." $22.00.

6" astronauts are all vinyl, multi-jointed. Part of the "Major Matt Mason" crew. Marked "1966/Mattel Inc./ U.S. & Foreign/Pat. Pending.

16" "Pulsar" comes "alive" when his back plate is pumped. Marked "Mattel Inc. 1976." $42.00.

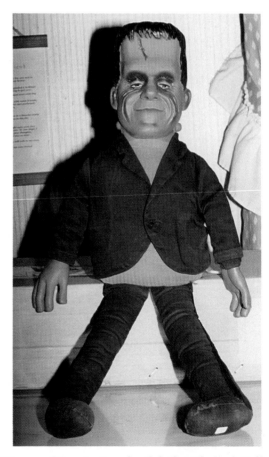

9" "Mork" (Robin Williams) talker. From TV's "Mork and Mindy." Marked "Mattel/1979/Paramount Pictures. $15.00.

21" "Herman Munster" made of cloth and vinyl. Pull string talker. Voice box in body. Made by Mattel in 1965. $50.00.

Left: 5½" "She-Ra, Princess of Power" – the most powerful women in the universe. Blonde hair. Molded white bodysuit. Gold cape attached to arms. Marked "Mattel Inc. 1984/Taiwan. Center: 5½" doll is one of the "Princess of Power" group. Pink/silver molded clothes and pink hair. Marked "M.I. 1984/Taiwan." Right: 5½" "Catra" is She-Ra's foe. Molded pink bodysuit and black hair. Marked "Mattel, Inc./1984/France." Each doll - $8.00.

Left: 11½" "Spectra" with pink and silver hair, vinyl head, and silver body. Lace dress. Marked "Mattel, Inc. 1986." Right: 12" "Tom Comet" is a friend of "Spectra." Has blue hair and silver body. Pink suit. Marked "Mattel, Inc. 1986." Each doll, mint condition - $35.00.

Left: 8" "Lady Lovelylocks" is made of plastic and vinyl with bend knees. Each doll in this group came with "pixietail" hairpieces. Marked "Mattel, Inc." Mint - $18.00. Right: 8" "Dutchess Raven Wave" has a pink and a lavender "pixietail" hairpiece. Marked "1986/T.C.F.C./M.A.C. Mattel, authorized user." $16.00.

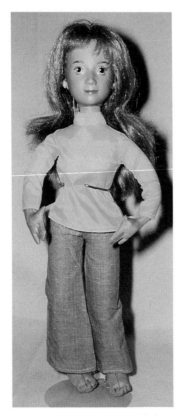

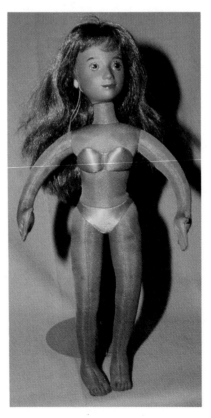

Left: 18" "Hot Looks" in original jeans and top. Vinyl head with stockinette limbs. Posable, stitched fingers. $65.00. Right: All the "Hot Looks" have sewn-on panties and bra. Nude - $35.00.

18" "Hot Looks International Teen Model." Vinyl with posable stockinette body and limbs. (Also came in black/brunette version.) Original. From 1987. $65.00.

15" "P.J. Sparkles" with plastic heart on chest. Beautiful painted eyes with sparkles. Plastic and vinyl. Battery operated. Marked "1988/Mattel Inc." $26.00.

13" "Little Miss Makeup" has painted makeup that appears with cold water; disappears with warm water. Original. Marked "Mattel, Inc. 1988–1977/Mexico" on head; "Mattel/Mexico" on body. $20.00.

15" "Baby Rose Tenderlove" made of plastic and vinyl with sleep eyes/lashes. Head marked "Mattel, Inc. 1988." $24.00.

21" "Baby Heather" of "Grow Up Series." Battery-operated cassette tape talker. Press patch on dress to change tape to grown up version. Marked "Mattel, Inc. 1987." $24.00.

Left: 12" "Captain Kirk" from *Star Trek - The Movie.* Original. Marked "Mego Corp./ 1977/Made in Hong Kong. $45.00.

Right: 12" "Spock" from *Star Trek - The Movie.* Marked "Mego Corp./1977/Made in Hong Kong." $48.00.

12½" "Superman" (left) and 12¼" "Spiderman" (right) are multi-jointed and made of plastic and vinyl. Both are original. Marked "D.C. Comics Inc. 1977" on head; "1978 Mego Corp." on back. Each - $25.00.

Left: 12" "The Incredible Hulk" figure made of plastic and vinyl with cloth pants. Marked "1978 Marvel Comics Group/All Rights Reserved/Made in Hong Kong. $15.00. Right: 10" "The Incredible Hulk" is unjointed but battery-operated string mechanism pulls weighted items up and down. Marked "1979 Marvel Comics Corp./Division of Cadence Industries/All Rights Reserved/1979/Mego Toys Inc./Made in Hong Kong." $18.00.

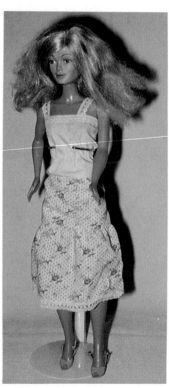

Left: 12½" "James Bond - 007" (Roger Moore) is multi-jointed action figure from movie *Moonraker*. Marked "1979 E.O.N./Productions/Ltd." on head and "Mego Corp. 1977/Made in Hong Kong" on body. $50.00. Center: 11½" "Little Candi" with full bangs and green painted eyes. Jointed waist, bendable knees. Marked "Mego Corp." on head and "Mego/1980/Made in Hong Kong" on back. $26.00. Right: 18" "Lady Linda" looks very much like the "Candi" doll. Tenon jointed arms, turn waist, side part hair. Original. Marked "1978 Mego." $45.00.

8" "Dukes of Hazzard" plastic and vinyl figures marked "1981 Mego." Men figures are multi-jointed. Left: "Boss Hogg" and "Bo." Right: "Daisy" has oversized head. Shown with "Luke." "Daisy" - $25.00; others - $23.00.

15" cloth and vinyl baby with sleep eyes and rooted hair. Made by Mego in 1978. $15.00.

17½" "Kelly" has sleep eyes/lashes and open/closed mouth. Battery operated. From 1980. Marked "60/Mego Corp." $14.00.

Left: Detail of 1988 Mel Appel Mannequin box. Mannequin in display stand has very attractive clothes. Set - $25.00. Right: "Mannequin" bride in stand. Figure is hollow plastic. $8.00.

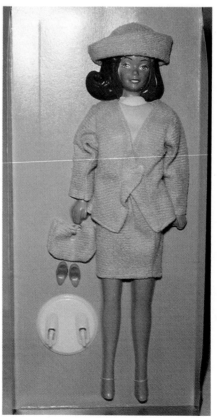
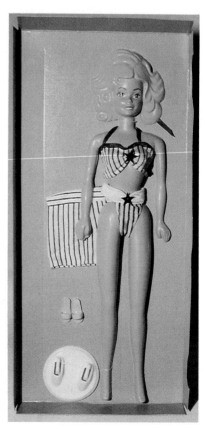

Left: Black evening dress is called "Night Mood." Center: Blue suit with hat and handbag. Right: Navy and white strip two-piece. Clothes fit all 11½" doll but were made especially for Mel Appel's "Model Collection." Each - $6.00 – 8.00.

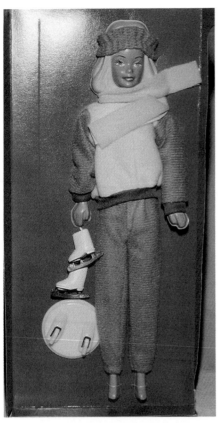
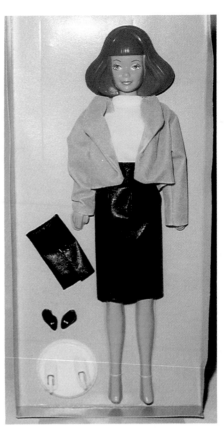
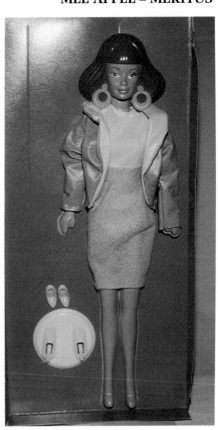

All three are mannequins for the 1988 Mel Appel "Model Collection." Snow/skate suit - $10.00; 2-piece pink and black suit - $8.00; Sheath and jacket - $6.00.

Above: 2" "Kidgetts Micro Fashions" doll. Fully jointed plus wrists. Painted features, rooted hair. Has molded-on undies and shoes. Marked "China" on leg and "1989" and "Meritus Industries/1989" on back. Complete - $8.00; Doll only - $2.00. Right: Shows doll with original packaging.

205

19" "Hide-A-Baby" is a cloth and vinyl doll with freckles on very character face and large oval painted eyes. Body has hidden pockets that contain a 3½" doll, a bead bracelet, and an elephant holding holding a package marked "Present." Head marked "Monarch Toy Co. Ltd." Tag marked "Hide-A-Baby/Pat./Pend/ 1986/Monarch Toy Co./All Rights Reserved." $90.00.

11" "Wizard" and "Dorothy" from *The Wizard of Oz*. Marked "1988 Turner Entertainment Co./Multi Toy Co." Each - $10.00.

Below: 11" "Tinman," "Scarecrow," and "Lion" from *The Wizard of Oz*. The lion has a cloth body with vinyl head and feet. Marked "1988 Turner Entertainment Co./Multi Toy Corp." Each - $10.00.

11" "Glenda, the Good Witch" and the evil "Wicked Witch of West" from *The Wizard of Oz*. Dolls marked "Turner Entertainment Co. 1988. Multi Toy Co." Each - $10.00.

Nancy Ann Storybook Dolls

Nancy Ann Storybook dolls take a lot of study unless they are found with original paper wrist tags and in correct marked original boxes. Many dolls have been placed in the wrong boxes, and the majority have the paper wrist tag torn off. The bisque dolls were made from 1937 to 1948. The plastic ones were made into the 1950s.

Allow more for unplayed with dolls and boxed dolls.

Bisque: 5" - $50.00 up; 7½−8" - $60.00 up. Jointed hips: 5" - $70.00; 7½−8" - $75.00 up. Swivel neck: 5" - $75.00; 7½−8" - $80.00 up. Swivel neck, jointed hips - $75.00 up. Black: 5" - $145.00; 7½−8" - $175.00. White painted socks - $160.00 up.

Plastic: 5" - $45.00; 7½−8" - $50.00−60.00.

5" bisque Nancy Ann Storybook doll in pink gown with lace trim. Mint - $65.00.

5" "Nancy Ann" made of plastic. Has sleep eyes and jointed neck. Burgandy gown and white apron with blue trim. Mint - $65.00.

4½" "Nancy Ann" made of plastic. Has sleep eyes. This is a reintroduced doll from early 1970s. Pink gown with blue trim. Marked "Storybook/Dolls/USA/Trademark/Reg. $25.00.

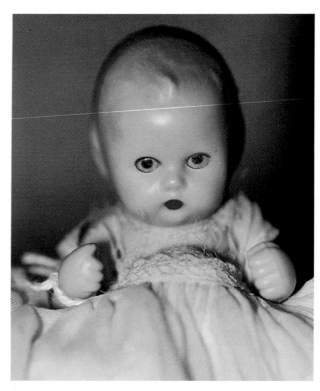

18" "Nancy Ann Style Show Doll" is all hard plastic and original. Has sleep eyes. Dolls are unmarked. $500.00 up.

3" "Nancy Ann" baby with sleep eyes. Dressed in original christening gown. From 1952. $85.00.

8" "Muffie" dolls made of all hard plastic with sleep eyes without eyebrows. All original. Left: Red hair doll with pink floral dress. Center: Blonde hair doll with pink/white striped dress and pink hat. Right: Black hair with purple/white stripe dress and white hat. Marked "Storybook Dolls/Calif." Each - $185.00 up.

8" "Muffie" dolls made of all hard plastic and all original. These dolls are walkers and have painted eyebrows. Left: Black hair doll with pink dress. Center: Brown hair doll with red body suit and blue sweater. Right: Blonde hair doll with blue/pink/white dress. Each - $185.00 up.

7½" "Muffie" with bend knees, unmarked. Box marked "Fairytale Dolls, Inc./San Francisco." $125.00.

10" "Nancy Ann" made of all vinyl with swivel waist, sleep eyes, and rooted hair. Original pink dress and silver shoes. Hat added. Marked on head. $90.00 up.

6" "Looking Pretty." Flat plastic body. Vinyl head with painted eyes and rooted hair. Press on and peel off clothes. Made in China by Ohio Art in 1988. $9.00.

11½" "Naomi" made of vinyl and plastic. Dressed in red/white striped blouse, blue skirt, and white/blue trim jacket. Extra clothes is black/white swimsuit. Made by Olmec Corp. in 1988. Box marked "Comic Corp. N.Y. America's Premier Black Toy Co." $50.00.

Left: 17" "Honeycomb" doll is made of plastic and vinyl with painted features and dimples. Excellent quality. Head marked "Panosh Place 1985. #10." Back marked "China." $52.00.

Right: 5" "Joan" is all vinyl with painted features and smile. Made in 1968. Marked "Perfekt. Hong Kong." $6.00.

Left: 5" "Milk Chocolate." Eyes painted closed. Original. Right: Shown in her box is 5" "Bon Bon." Both are plastic and vinyl and marked "1981 (or 1983) Phoenix Toys, Inc." Others in set were "Chocolate Russe," "Dixie Bell Cupper," "Eclair," "Mellow Roll," and "Sugar Cane." Each - $7.00.

27" "Cricket" is a battery-operated talker. Black version. Eyes and mouth move. Original and sitting in original chair. Marked "9250/Playmate/1985." $185.00.

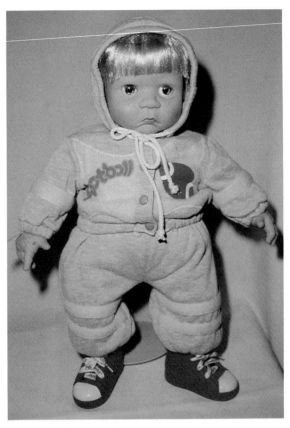

22" pouty from the "Tiara Dolls Series." Made of cloth and vinyl. Sleep eyes, rooted hair. Original. Marked "Playmate/1986." $34.00.

14" "Grow Up Doll" that grows when crank is turned on back. Plastic and vinyl with painted eyes. Marked "Playmates 1987." $30.00.

Left: 15" "Dick Tracy" has molded-on clothes and removable yellow trench coat. Based on Warren Beatty's character in *Dick Tracy* movie. Made by Playmate in 1990. Unmarked. $15.00.

Right: 14" "Breathless Mahoney" has molded-on blue gown, removable blue boa. Vinyl head, rooted hair, and painted earrings. Based on Madonna's character in *Dick Tracy* movie. Made by Playmate in 1990. $15.00.

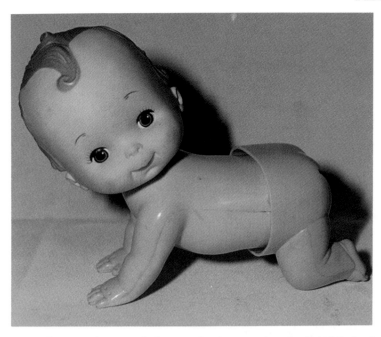

8" "Baby Crawl Around" has a plastic two-piece body and vinyl head. Battery-operated. Marked "9076/Playmate 1981/Hong Kong." $10.00.

33" "Jill" record player talker. Eyes, mouth, and hand moves. Multi-jointed. Marked "Playskool Inc. 1987/900/23." $200.00 up.

13" "Jammie Pies" in original blue and orange trim outfit. Cloth body, stockinette style face with painted features and hair. Name imprinted on foot. $12.00.

213

7½" "Sweetie Pops" is molded on her knees in one piece. Has molded-on undies. Clothes come with arms and legs attached and makes her into a standing doll. Marked "Playskool 1986, Sub. Hasbro." $18.00. Below: Shows doll in one of her dresses.

9½" "Dolly Surprise" dolls are made of all vinyl with painted features. Arm functions cause hair to "grow" or shorten. Left: "Tuck Me In" doll. Marked "Playskool 1988" on head. Right: "Rain Dancer" doll. Marked "1989 Playskool." Each - $18.00.

6½" "Little Miss Dolly Surprise." Raise right arm and hair grows; left arm makes it shorter. Plastic/vinyl with painted-on long white stockings and purple slippers. Wears "Spring Fling" outfit. Made by Playskool, 1989. $16.00.

15" "Baby Doll Surprise" has pink plastic ring in top of head. Raise right arm and hair grows; left arm makes it shorter. Large painted eyes. Original. Marked "1988 Playskool, Inc." on head. $20.00.

10" and 5" "Baby Betty Boop" is all vinyl with painted features. Original. Dog marked "Marty Toy" named "Midgey." Marked "1987 King Features. Made by Presents, 1986." 10" - $16.00; 5" $12.00.

11" "Popeye" made of cloth and vinyl. Has one piece of hair and cotton "smoke" from pipe. Vinyl head with molded-on cap and vinyl arms. Marked "Presents. Div. of Hamilton Gifts. King Features, 1985." $22.00.

15" "Lion" from *The Wizard of Oz*. Plush with imbedded whiskers and vinyl face. Wears metal "Badge of Courage." Tagged "Exclusive by Presents. Division of Hamilton Gifts. Copyright 1939. Loew's Inc. Ren. 1966. Metro-Goldwyn-Mayer, Inc. All Rights Reserved. 1987 Turner Entertainment Co. Made in China." $20.00.

17" "Precious Moments" named "Debbie." Porcelain and cloth doll from 1980. $165.00 up.

8" Indian "Precious Moments" made of all rigid vinyl. Marked "Made in Phillipines/Precious Moments/by Samuel/ Butcher Co./U.S.A. 1989." $36.00.

15" "Precious Moments – Silent Night Collection." All cloth with painted features. Tagged "Samuel J. Butcher. Applause. 1989." Set. $95.00 up.

11" "Elvis" made of plastic and vinyl. Very life-like. White jumpsuit with eagle design and gold belt. (Was available in several different outfits.) Marked "1984 endorsed by Graceland. Produced by Eugene Doll Co., Inc. 1984 E.P.E., Inc." $35.00 up.

Raggedy Ann & Andy

Raggedy Ann and Andy dolls, books, and other collectibles have become very highly prized by collectors, and because of the interest in these items, the prices have soared. Raggedy Ann and Andy items are extremely difficult to find, but the search is fun!

Early Raggedy Ann and Andy dolls will be marked "Patented Sept. 7, 1915." Volland Company made the dolls from 1920 to 1934. During the mid to late 1930s Raggedy Ann and Andy were made by Georgene Averill and Mollye Dolls. Later, they were made by Knickerbocker Toy Company from 1963 and 1982. Since 1983, Applause has produced this delightful pair and they are still very popular with children – and collectors.

20" and 30" Raggedy Ann & Andy. These early examples have oil-painted features and socks. Clothes most likely replacements. Shown with 22" baby made of composition and cloth with tin sleep eyes. Open mouth with two front teeth. Ca. early 1930s. Unmarked. Raggedy Ann - $1,000.00; Raggedy Andy - $900.00; 22" - $40.00.

"Raggedy Ann & Andy" made by Volland. "Andy" is from the 1920s. "Ann" is stamped with date "1915." Each - $800.00 up.

6" and 18" "Raggedy Ann & Andy" are all original and made by Knickerbocker. Even the Knickerbocker dolls are getting hard to find. 6", each - $12.00; 18", each - $60.00.

20" "Raggedy Ann & Andy." "Dress-me" dolls with belt, buckles, buttons, and ties. Helps children to learn to dress themselves. Each - $85.00.

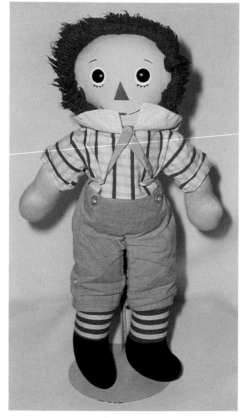

Left: 24" "Raggedy Ann" has zipper, button, ties, and is a teaching doll to show child how to operate these items. Oilcloth shoes. Original. Has a Knickerbocker tag. $85.00. Right: 16" "Raggedy Andy" All original. Made by Knickerbocker, ca. 1982. $35.00.

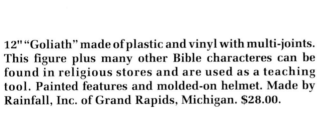

"Raggedy Ann and Andy" books published by Bobbs-Merrell, 1961. Each - $30.00 – 75.00 up.

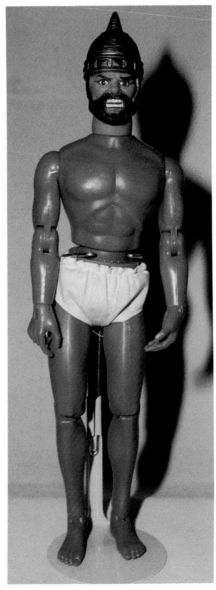

12" "Goliath" made of plastic and vinyl with multi-joints. This figure plus many other Bible characteres can be found in religious stores and are used as a teaching tool. Painted features and molded-on helmet. Made by Rainfall, Inc. of Grand Rapids, Michigan. $28.00.

5" "Monkees" (Mickey, Peter, and Davy) finger puppets. Half of doll is suit with plastic boots for child's fingers to go into legs. Offered through Kellogg's and also sold in stores with fourth member, Mike. Marked "1970/Remco Ind. Inc. Harrison N.J. Pat. Pend. Hong Kong." Paper label: "1970" and "TM of Columbia Pictures Ind., Inc. Remco Authorized user. Made in Hong Kong." Set - $45.00 up.

14" "Brown Eye Billy" made of plastic and vinyl with sleep eyes. Original. Made by Remco. From 1970s. $30.00.

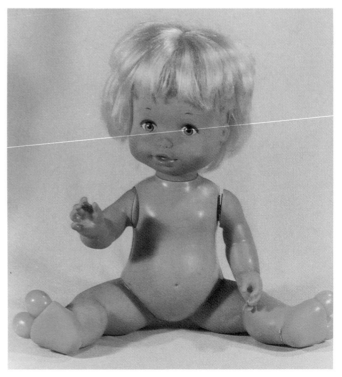

13" "Baby This 'n That" has two types of vinyl used – one for skull cap; one for rest of doll. Two large toes on each foot. Press toes to make actions. Two styles of joints at shoulders. Nude doll above shows different shoulder joints and large toes. Marked "Remco 1976" on head and "Remco Toys Inc./New York N.Y. 10010/Made in Hong Kong/Patent Pending/Pro." on body. $38.00.

14" "Yes–No" doll is plastic and vinyl with painted features. Button on back makes head move. Marked "1978 Remco N.Y. N.Y." $29.00.

14" plastic and vinyl child is battery operated and an open mouth nurser. Note very stubby fingers. Marked "Remco 1979" on head and "Remco 1979/Pat. Pend. Made in Hong Kong" on back. $28.00.

8" "Sandra Sue" dolls made of all hard plastic with walker legs. (Head does not turn.) Excellent quality doll and clothes. Made by Richwood in 1950s. Each - $85.00.

Two 8" "Sandra Sue" shown in different outfits. Above photo shows original box and list of clothes made for doll. $85.00 up.

Dolls made by Roberta Doll Co. Left: 17" "Roberta Walker" made of all hard plastic with sleep eyes, glued-on wig, open mouth, and saran hair. Original except for sash and shoes. 1955. $65.00 up. Center: 19" "Roberta Fashion" made of plastic and vinyl with sleep eyes, rooted hair, and high heel feet. Original red dress with silver bow and shoes. Will be unmarked or marked "AE" plus number. 1958. $55.00 up. Right: 24" "Roberta Ann" is all original in original box. Vinyl head with rooted hair, sleep eyes, one-piece vinyl body and limbs. Wide open/closed mouth. 1953. $65.00.

From Dogpatch, home of Lil' Abner and Daisy came the "Shmoos" in the late 1940s. These have become very collectible and difficult to find. Shown is a figurine, a vinyl decal, a plush toy, and salt & pepper shakers. $15.00 up.

9½" "Shmoo" all vinyl squeeze toy. Marked on bottom "1976 Annette Tison and Talus Taylor. All Rights Reserved. Barbapappa™ Doll/A License of FFP Licensing North America Inc./Made in U.S.A. Shellcore Inc." $18.00.

Right: Different set of "Shmoo" salt & pepper shakers. He has blue/white stripe collar, and she has green bow. Both have modeled-on features. Set - $15.00.

Below: Box with original "Shmoo" soap. Each have painted features. $30.00.

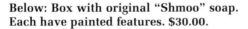

Three different 16" "Kim" dolls in outfits that reflect the time period that the doll was made. Both black and white dolls were available. Made from 1969 – 1973. Marked "Shindana Dolls." Each - $35.00.

18" "Shirley Temple" dolls made of all composition. Left to right: "Merrily Yours" has red star print dress. "Our Little Girl" has blue dress with white music note. "Baby Take A Bow" has red polka dot dress. "Baby Take A Bow" has pale blue pleated dress. "Our Little Girl" has red dress with white Scotty dogs on front. "Curly Top" has peach print dress. "Bright Eyes" has plaid dress. Each - $725.00 up.

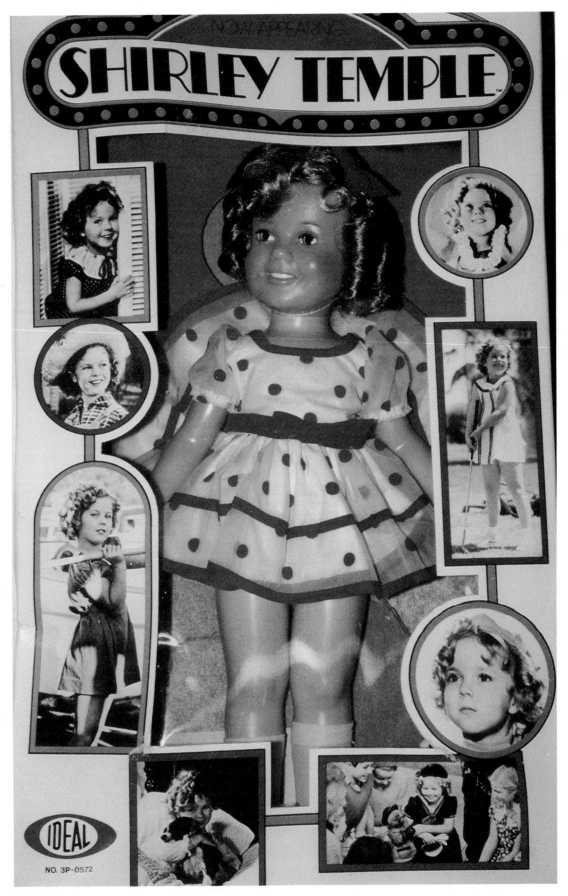

17" "Shirley Temple" made of plastic and vinyl, shown in original box. Many of doll collectors feel this particular "Shirley" resembles best the child star. From 1973 – 1974. In box - $165.00 up; Doll only - $95.00 up.

Above: 36" "Shirley Temple" made of vinyl with sleep eyes. Still has factory hairpins in hair. All original with original dress pin. Marked "ST36–38–2" on head and "G–36–7" on back. $150.00 up.

Left: 16" "Shirley Temple Baby" with flirty sleep eyes. Open mouth with upper and lower teeth. Cloth body, composition head, shoulder plate, and limbs. Original. $950.00 up.

Left: 12" "Shirley Temple" double-packed dolls. Includes dolls, dress, raincoat, cap, tote bag, slip, and pajamas. From 1960. Right: Shows box that holds dolls and clothes. Set - $200.00.

15" "Shirley Temple" dolls made of all vinyl. Left to right: red sailor dress, Red Riding Hood, Bo Peep, and pink party dress. From 1958. Each - $265.00 up.

Above: Shirley Temple Glamour Girl set has two pump bottles. Made by Gabriel in 1959. $45.00 up.

Right: Rare Shirley Temple pin about the size of a doll's button. Wording on edge reads "Shirley Temple's Pet Rowdy." $60.00.

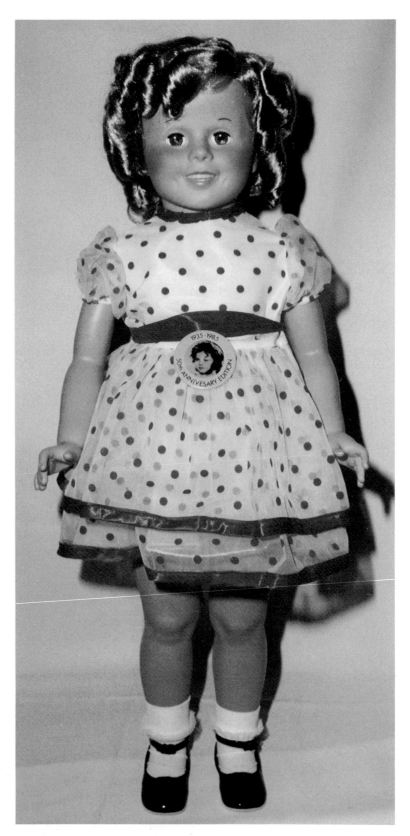

36" "Shirley Temple" with orange skin tone. Marketed in 1985 by company owned and operated by Hank Garfinkle, the past research and development manager for the Ideal Toy Corp. after it was purchased by C.B.S. Marked "17/1984 Mrs. Shirley Temple Black/Dolls Dreams and Love." $195.00.

8" plush figures from Showbiz Pizza Place – "Billie Bob," "Ralph," "Mitzi," and drum playing "Fatz." All were made in Taiwan in 1980s. Each - $22.00.

29" football and baseball players made of composition and cloth with painted smiling features and painted hair. Football player has cleats. Original from 1935. Both are marked "Sterling Doll Co." Each - $245.00.

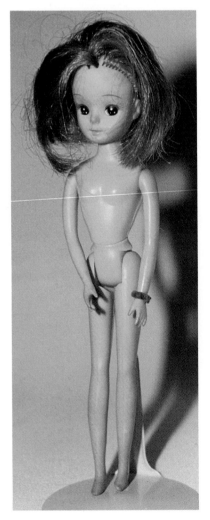

8" plastic and vinyl teen doll with bend knees and jointed waist. Round eyes with three different iris colors. Similar to the "Japanese Barbie" made for children of Japan. Marked "Takara/Made in Japan." $12.00.

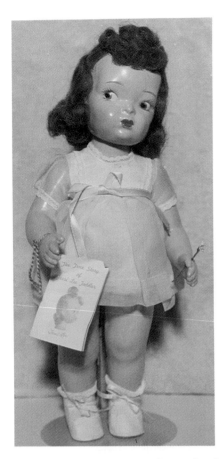

17" "Terri Lee" is all composition and completely original. Brown eyes are painted to the side. 1947 – 1949. $350.00.

16" "Terri Lee" with marked head and body. 1951. $285.00 up. 10" "Tiny Terri Lee" walker with sleep eyes. 1956. $175.00 up. 10" "Linda Baby" is all vinyl with molded hair and painted features. 1951. $185.00 up.

"Terri Lee" wardrobe measures 17" x 10" x 7" and made of all natural wood. Painted trim on front with "Terri Lee" name and initials. Sticker on inside door reads "TM Reg. U.S. Pat. Off. Scandia Toys Los Angles" with emblem of a Viking ship. Plastic hangers imprinted "Terri Lee Apple Valley California, Ca." Ca. 1950. $200.00.

18" "Connie Lynn" with curved baby legs, caracul wig, and long lashes. Original romper suit tagged and has original soft vinyl baby booties with embossed flowers and bows. 1955. $375.00.

16" "Terri Lee" is very pretty in one of her many coats that were sold boxed separately. Shoes replaced. $285.00 up.

27" "Cindy Snow" made of all white plush with vinyl head. Face mask has painted features. From early 1950s. Tagged "Timely Toys." Above is full head shot of doll. It is not known if she is an advertising item or a "play" doll. $250.00 up.

26" "Cindy Snow" with plush, unjointed body. Early vinyl head and hands. Eyes painted in squinted position. Tuff of nylon hair with plush back. Inside of pockets match the scarf and cap trim. Tagged "Timely Toys." Sled from 1940s and doll from 1950s. $250.00 up.

17" "Kimberly" made of plastic and vinyl with painted features and rooted hair. Came with smile and closed mouth versions. Doll on left has pink gown called "Getting Fancy." Doll is marked "1984 Tomy" but was on market as late as 1989. Each - $45.00.

13" babies made of all vinyl with painted features. Doll on left has green hair; the one on the right has gray hair. Marked "Tonka 1985. Made in China." Each - $20.00.

5" "Hollywoods" with blue hair that changes colors. Molded-on sunglasses, swimsuit, and sandals. Six in sets are "Holly," "Molly," "Dolly," "Polly," "Jill," and "Jackie" (shown). Made by Tonka in 1984. $16.00.

11½" "Marilyn Monroe" has all vinyl construction with painted features and jointed waist. Her green dress is from her movie *Let's Make It Legal*. Marked "Tri-Star 1982 Twentieth Century Fox Corp." $35.00.

16½" "Marilyn Monroe" is all vinyl with painted features. Her white dress is from her movie *Seven Year Itch.* Box marked "1982." Doll marked "Twentieth Century Fox Corp. Tri-Star International, Ltd." $85.00.

11½" "Winter Wonderland Sandi," a limited edition doll. Blue sparkle gown, lace sleeves. Marked "1987 Totsy." $30.00.

4" "Miss Butterfly" is an all vinyl teen doll with swivel waist. Attached to butterfly pillow. One of the four "Satin Sweetheart" series dolls. Marked on back "Toytime/Inc/ N.Y./1981/H.K. $14.00.

8" Troll bank with inset eyes. All original, 1960s. $32.00.

Right: 5" Troll made of all vinyl with inset eyes. Hair has been trimmed. Original. $22.00.

3½" "Bike Nik" Wishnik. One-piece body and head. Black hair, inset eyes. By Uneeda in 1982. $15.00.

12" Troll giraffe with inset eyes and jointed neck. Marked "Thomas Dam/Made in Denmark" on bottom of foot. $70.00.

3" Troll with inset eyes. Made by Uneeda, from 1960s. Marked with horseshoes on feet. $18.00.

Left: 3" "Super Troll" with brown inset eyes and white hair. Molded and painted-on red/white clothing. $18.00. Right: 5" long Troll turtle. Very rare animal troll. Marked "DAM-1964." $60.00.

Trolls were reintroduced in the mid-1980s. By the late 1980s and into the 1990s, the "Norfin Troll" came on the market. The faces are not exactly the same as the original Trolls but similar. The vinyl is a different material altogether. $12.00.

4½" "Wishnik" is bendable. Dressed in tennis outfit. Red hair and inset eyes. Figure is more flat than round. Made by Uneeda. Marked "MCMLXXVII (1977) Brooklyn." In package - $35.00; Troll only - $18.00.

9" Norfin Troll made of all vinyl and called "Lil' Nighty." Made in Denmark by Dam Things APS. Imported by E.F.S. $22.00.

Left: 8" "Ariel, The Little Mermaid" comes with extra outfit. Marked "Disney. Made in Hong Kong. Made by Tyco. 1990." Right: 12" "Eric" is Ariel's prince from the movie *The Little Mermaid*. Marked "Disney" on head and "Hong Kong. Made by Tyco. 1990" on back. Each - $28.00.

2½" "Quints" with molded-on diapers. Painted features, rooted hair, and fully jointed. Babies numbered 1 – 5 in hearts on back of diapers. Marked "Tyco. 1990." Set - $15.00.

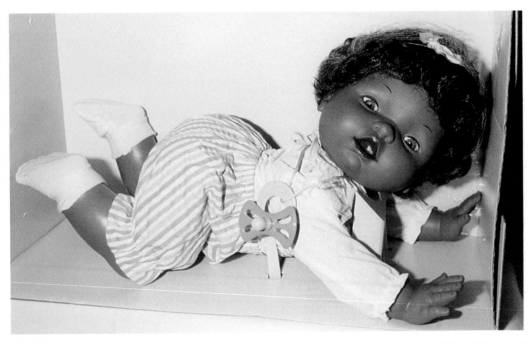

17" "Oopsie Daisy" is a battery-operated crawler with painted features. Jointed shoulders and neck. Unjointed bent legs. Doll cries and head moves when she crawls. Black and white versions available. Made by Tyco in 1989. $45.00.

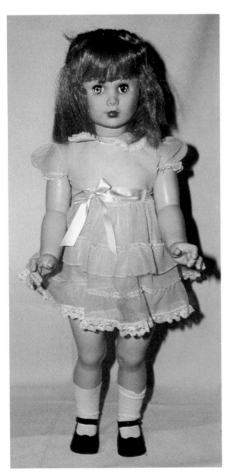

Left: 34" "Stella Walker" with sleep eyes and body like Ideal's "Patty Playpal" and "Shirley Temple." Made by Uneeda Doll Co. in 1960. Marked "U" on head. $95.00.

Right: 32" "Fairy Princess" is dressed in pink ballerina outfit with silver trim. Sleep eyes, pink rooted hair. Extra joint at wrist and waist. From Walt Disney's *Babes in Toyland*. This doll with different costume and hair color was used as "Pollyanna." $145.00.

21" "Wiggles Kid" made of plastic and vinyl with open mouth and two upper teeth. Marked "Uneeda, 1964." $38.00.

18" "Minuette Baby" made of plastic and vinyl with open mouth. Right arm bent at elbow so thumb will go in mouth. Has sleep eyes and rooted hair. Marked "Uneeda Doll Co., Inc. 1969/18-BL" $25.00.

14" "Jennifer" fashion doll with sleep eyes/lashes and long thin fingers. Also came in 17" size. From 1972–1973. Marked "Uneeda Doll Co., Inc./MCMLXXII/Made in Hong Kong." $27.00.

9½" "Tummy, the Pudgy Pixie" is made of plastic and vinyl with painted features. Marked "Uneeda Doll Co., Inc. 1972." $18.00.

Left: 13" "Plummie Splash" made of all vinyl with painted features and red molded hair. Has "flat" face. Marked "Uneeda Doll Co., Inc. 214/MCMLXXIV (1974)." $14.00.

Right: 13" "Granny" from "Granny & Me" set. Has missing bonnet that was made from the same material as dress pocket. Her glasses are painted on. Earlier version of this doll had round painted-on glasses. Came with 7" "Me" doll that was dressed in reversed – multi-print gown and plain brown apron. Marked "Uneeda" or "U.C.C., Inc. 1977." $18.00.

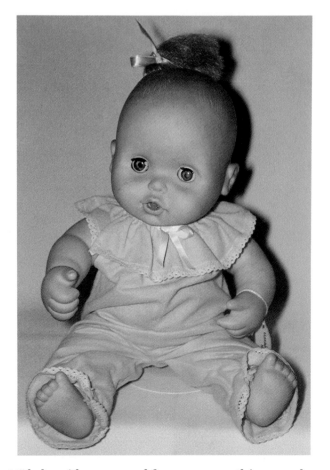

14" cloth and vinyl doll with sleep eyes and freckles. Open/closed mouth with painted upper teeth. Braids in hair. Marked "U.D.C., Inc. Made in China. 1979." $12.00.

14" baby with very round face, open mouth/nurser, sleep eyes, and one tuff of rooted hair. Marked "Uneeda Doll Co., Inc. 1984." $18.00.

12" "Baby Bee" is a plastic and vinyl baby with sleep eyes, open mouth/nurser. Marked "U.D.C., Inc./MCLMXXXIV (1984). Made in China." $10.00.

15" "Littlest Angel" made of plastic and vinyl with green sleep eyes, red hair, and freckles. Original tagged clothes. Made after Vogue Doll was sold to Lesney of England and Lesney sold to Tonka Corp. Marked "Vogue Dolls, Inc. 1965." Box marked "Melrose Tonka Corp." $30.00.

"Dutch," "Tyrolean," and "Polish" dolls from the "Ginny of Faraway Lands" series. Made of vinyl with sleep eyes and rooted hair. From 1965. Each - $50.00.

14" "Lil Imp" made of plastic and vinyl with round sleep eyes and red rooted hair. Shown with original box and pamphlet. Marked "Vogue Doll 1964." $65.00 up.

Left: 8" "Toodles" made of all composition with painted features. Original "Uncle Sam" outfit with gold paper label on pants leg. From 1940s. $295.00 up. Right: 14" "Mary Jane" made of all composition. Pink dress, blue coat with fur trim, and blue/white tam. Clothes are tagged. Doll was supplied by Ideal for Vogue to dress. Made in 1947. Unmarked. $345.00 up.

Left: 8" "Ginny Baby" made of all vinyl with painted eyes and molded hair. Open mouth/nurser. $60.00. Right: 8" "Ginny" made of all hard plastic. Original except for shoes. From early 1950s. $265.00 up. Seated in high chair is "Ginny Baby" made of all vinyl with sleep eyes. Original, early 1950s. $60.00.

Close-up of brother and sister "Ginny." Painted lashes and eyebrows. Outfits are red and red/blue plaid. They are #35 and #36 called "Steve" and "Eve." From 1952. $285.00 up.

"Ginny" with sleep eyes and painted lashes. Jointed knee walker. Original clothes but hat is missing. $265.00 up.

7½" "Ginny" made of all hard plastic with painted eyes. Original. From 1949. Marked "Vogue" on head and "Vogue Doll" on back. $350.00 up.

Close-up of "Ginny" made of hard plastic with painted eyes. Ca. 1948 – 1950. $350.00 up.

16" "Brickette" with mod red hair and sleep eyes. Original. Marked "Lesney Prod. Corp. 1978/71679" on head. Dress tagged "Vogue Dolls, Inc. Made in U.S.A." $95.00.

8" "Ginny Sasson Doll." Original. This style was made through 1980. Marked "Ginny/Vogue Dolls/1977." $60.00.

11" "Baby Wide Eyes" made of plastic and vinyl with sleep eyes, open mouth/nurser, and rooted over molded hair. Sold through 1982. Marked "Vogue 1975" on head. $30.00.

8" "Ginny" made of all vinyl with sleep eyes. All original in red coat and bonnet. Marked "Ginny" on head and "Vogue Inc./Mil. 1984/Hong Kong" on back. $50.00 up.

12" "My Baby" was also marketed as "Ginny Baby." Sleep eyes, open mouth/nurser. This original doll is from 1982. Marked "Vogue" on head. $22.00.

"Ginny" made for Shirley's Doll House of Wheeling, Illinois. Quality of doll and clothes are excellent. Shown with miniature horses, the personal hobby of Shirley Bertrand, owner of store. 1986 exclusive. $165.00 up.

Left: 11½" "Precious Picture" of the "Posing Picture Perfect Dolls." Other dolls in set are "Penny" in majorette outfit and "Perky Pip" (right) in white outfit. Applied earrings, bend knees. Battery operated dolls have cut out space in back to plug into base which is operated by micro floppy disc. Came with real 110 camera and photo album. Distributed by Wonderama in 1990. Dolls marked "Henry Garfinkle." $75.00.

"Penny" of "Posing Picture Perfect Dolls" designed by Henry Garfinkle. Dolls distributed by Wonderama. $75.00.

5" "Snidley" from the "Rocky and Bullwinkle" cartoons. Fully posable and dressed in black. Marked "Snidley/ Wham-o Mfg./1972/Pat. Jay World Productions/Made in Hong Kong." $12.00.

14" "Lady Elaine" has green painted eyes and mauve/ gold outfit. From "Camelot Series" by Robin Woods, 1989. $165.00.

Left: 14" "Young Merlin" with freckles and smiling closed mouth. Dressed in royal blue and silver wizard outfit. Right: 14" "Lady Linet" with painted features. Peach and green outfit. Both dolls are from "Camelot Series" by Robin Woods, 1989. Each - $165.00.

14" "Lady of the Lakes" is one of prettiest dolls in the "Camelot Series." Blue and silver outfit with net holding lobster and starfish. Green eyes. Made by Robin Woods, 1989. $200.00 up.

14" "Morgana" with black hair and elaborate red/gold gown. Doll and clothing are of excellent quality. From "Camelot Series" by Robin Woods, 1989. $200.00 up.

14" "Juliet" made of plastic and vinyl with painted features. Dressed in red/gold/white gown. All original. $185.00 up.

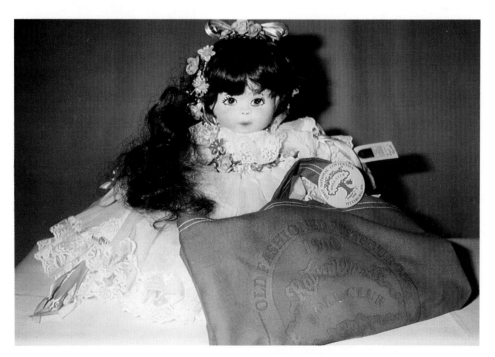

19" "Sarah Elizabeth" dressed in white with flower and lace tirm. She is the first Robin Woods' Club doll, from 1990. Shown here with tote bag. $300.00 up.

These 18" "Elvis" dolls are excellent examples of the "King" and highly collectible. Left: "Elvis" dressed in "The Flame" outfit. Third in series. Right: "Elvis" dressed in black and called "The Phoenix." Made by World Doll. Each - $95.00 up.

11½" "Elizabeth Taylor" in white dress from her movie *Cat on Hot Tin Roof*. Limited edition marked "World Doll." Box marked "1858 Loews, Inc. & Avon Products. 1985 M.G.M./U.A. Entertainment/1988 Turner Entertainment Co. All Rights Reserves." $40.00.

12" "Scarlett" and "Rhett Butler" made of vinyl and plastic with painted features. Made by World Dolls. Each - $45.00.

11½" "Scarlett in Red" in red gown trimmed in feathers. Painted eyes and green eyeshadow. Made by World Doll in 1990. Marked "1939 Selnick, Ren. 1967 MGM World Doll." $40.00.

Left: 11½" "Ashley" in gray Confederate uniform trimmed in gold. Right: 11½" "Melanie" in light blue dress with peach ribbon sash and hat ribbons. Both were made in 1990 and marked the same as Scarlett doll above. Each - $40.00.

21" "Pamela" has vinyl head and limbs with cloth body. Sleep eyes with painted lashes on top and bottom. Battery- operated talker that responds to touch. Comes with different outfits, books, and talking devices. Marked "1986 Pamela/Worlds of Wonder, Inc./Patent Pending." $180.00 up.

Index

261

Schroeder's
ANTIQUES
Price Guide

. . . is the #1 best-selling antiques & collectibles value guide on the market today, and here's why . . .

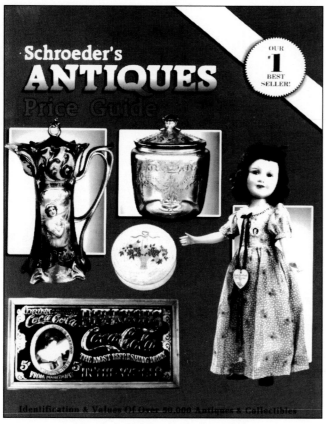

8½ x 11, 608 Pages, $12.95

• *More than 300 advisors, well-known dealers, and top-notch collectors work together with our editors to bring you accurate information regarding pricing and identification.*

• *More than 45,000 items in almost 500 categories are listed along with hundreds of sharp original photos that illustrate not only the rare and unusual, but the common, popular collectibles as well.*

• *Each large close-up shot shows important details clearly. Every subject is represented with histories and background information, a feature not found in any of our competitors' publications.*

• *Our editors keep abreast of newly-developing trends, often adding several new categories a year as the need arises.*

If it merits the interest of today's collector, you'll find it in *Schroeder's*. And you can feel confident that the information we publish is up to date and accurate. Our advisors thoroughly check each category to spot inconsistencies, listings that may not be entirely reflective of market dealings, and lines too vague to be of merit. Only the best of the lot remains for publication.

Without doubt, you'll find
SCHROEDER'S ANTIQUES PRICE GUIDE
the only one to buy for
reliable information and values.

COLLECTOR BOOKS
A Division of Schroeder Publishing Co., Inc.